new and selected poems

new
and
selected
poems

cecilia vicuña

Edited and translated by **Rosa Alcalá**

Additional translations by Esther Allen, Suzanne Jill Levine, Edwin Morgan, Urayoán Noel, James O'Hern, Anne Twitty, Eliot Weinberger, and Christopher Winks

Introduction by **Daniel Borzutzky**

Published by **Kelsey Street Press**

Kelsey Street Press

2824 Kelsey St., Berkeley, CA 94705

info@kelseyst.com

www.kelseyst.com

ISBN 978-0-932716-87-3

Designed by Quemadura

Acknowledgments

Cecilia Vicuña: Special thanks to Rosa Alcalá for a lifetime of poetic work alongside mine; thanks to Kelsey Street Press, Rena Rosenwasser, Anna Morrison, and the whole team for believing in this work; and to James O'Hern for his unfailing support, love, and vision.

Rosa Alcalá: My contributions to this book were made possible by a Literary Translation Fellowship from the National Endowment for the Arts and a research leave granted by the University of Texas at El Paso. I am also indebted to Carmen Giménez Smith, Jen Hofer, Daniel Borzutzky, Kristin Dykstra, and Jeff Sirkin for their generous and astute insights. Special thanks to Cecilia Vicuña for her trust in me. And to my fellow translators in this book, my utmost admiration. The editor and author gratefully acknowledge the following presses and journals:

Saborami was first published by Beau Geste Press, 1973, Devon, England. It was also published by ChainLinks, 2011, Oakland, CA, and Philadelphia, PA.

PALABRAR*mas* was first published by El Imaginero, 1984, Buenos Aires, Argentina.

Precario/Precarious, translated by Anne Twitty, was first published by Tanam Press, 1983, New York, NY.

La Wik'uña was first published by Francisco Zegers, Editor, 1990, Santiago, Chile.

Unravelling Words & the Weaving of Water, translated by Eliot Weinberger and Suzanne Jill Levine, was first published by Graywolf Press, 1992, Minneapolis, MN. That book includes selections from *Precario*, PALABRAR*mas*, and *La Wik'uña*, along with new work. Translations © 1992 by Eliot Weinberger and Suzanne Jill Levine.

Word & Thread was first published as an artist's book during the exhibition *Cecilia Vicuña—Precario: Words & Thread* (Inverleith House, Royal Botanic Garden, Edinburgh, Scotland, October 26, 1996–January 5, 1997).

Palabra e hilo/Word & Thread, translated by Rosa Alcalá, was published by Morning Star Publications, 1997, Edinburgh, Scotland.

Cloud-net was published as a book-catalog of the installation that traveled to Hallwalls Contemporary Arts Center in Buffalo, New York; Art in General in Brooklyn, NY; and DiverseWorks in Houston, TX (1999–2000).

El Templo, translated by Rosa Alcalá, was first published by Situations Press, 2001, New York, NY.

QUIPOem/The Precarious: The Art and Poetry of Cecilia Vicuña, edited by M. Catherine de Zegher and translated by Esther Allen, was first published by Wesleyan University Press, 1997, Middletown, CT.

Instan was first published by Kelsey Street Press, 2002, Berkeley, CA.

Spit Temple: The Selected Performances of Cecilia Vicuña, edited and translated by Rosa Alcalá, was first published by Ugly Duckling Presse, 2012, Brooklyn, NY.

From Uncollected Poems: "Libro Desierto/Desert Book" was first published in *A Book of the Book: Some Works & Projections about the Book & Writing*, edited by Jerome Rothenberg and Steven Clay, Granary Books, 2000, New York. "Disprosodias Xul Solar y el I Ching/ Disprosodies Xul Solar and the I Ching" was first published in *Rattapallax* and also appeared in the exhibition catalog *Xul Solar and Jorge Luis Borges: The Art of Friendship*, 2013, co-presented by Americas Society, Fundación Pan Klub-Museo Xul Solar, and Fundación Internacional Jorge Luis Borges. "The Melody of Structures" was first published in *3X Abstraction: New Methods of Drawing by Hilma af Klint, Emma Kunz, and Agnes Martin*, 2005, The Drawing Center, Yale University Press, New York, NY.

We dedicate this book to the memory of

Dennis Tedlock,

teacher and friend, whose unparalleled contributions to the translation and study of Amerindian poetics inspired and guided us.

Contents

Stupid Diary/Sabor a Mí 1966–1971

PALABRAR*mas* 1966–2015

Precarious/Precario 1966–2015

The Vicuña/La Wik'uña

QUIPOem/The Precarious: The Art and Poetry of Cecilia Vicuña

Instan

Spit Temple

Uncollected Poems

Performance Notes

No, No, and No
The Art of Cecilia Vicuña

Daniel Borzutzky

1

I saw Cecilia Vicuña perform a few weeks ago. She tied us up.

This was a site-specific performance at the Poetry Foundation in Chicago as part of *Dianna Frid and Cecilia Vicuña: A Textile Exhibition*.

As she came into the theater, she unspooled the red yarn, silently asking different audience members to hold onto pieces. And when the yarn was completely unraveled, when we had sat in silence with it for a few minutes, she made a wavelike motion with her hands that asked us to jubilantly shake the yarn above our heads.

Backtrack:

My eight-year-old son, Lorenzo, is holding a piece of yarn above his head. He is sitting on the border of the aisle that separates the two sides of the theater. The yarn traverses the theater. It binds two men sitting across from us. Lorenzo lets go of his piece for a moment, skips toward me, and says, "Wouldn't it be awesome if we tried to run through the yarn?"

And it would be awesome. And my guess is that Vicuña wouldn't have minded if he had attempted to run through the maze of red. In fact, as we walked into the Poetry Foundation, Vicuña greeted Lorenzo with an invitation.

"I will start doing something, but I don't know what I will do. As I start doing it, do you want to do it with me?"

Lorenzo was feeling shy and declined the invitation, but I was struck, nevertheless, by its spontaneity, its offer to cede control to the whims of an eight-year-old, to give the eight-year-old the spotlight and the power to create and own the art with and alongside her.

Vicuña's art is constantly offering these types of invitations: to inhabit it, to touch it, to modify it, to run wildly through it, and to tiptoe carefully in order to experience the nuances of every turn and angle we must navigate—and it has been doing so for almost 50 years.

In her 1973 collection, *Saborami*, originally published in England by Mexican artist Felipe Ehrenberg's Beau Geste Press as an artist's book with a run of 250 copies, there are several pages of journal entries Vicuña wrote about an early and important art event called "Otoño/Autumn":

> In June 1971 I filled with autumn leaves a room
> at the national fine arts museum in Santiago,
> in collaboration with claudio bertoni and nemesio
> antúnez. . . . this piece was conceived as a contribution
> to socialism in Chile.

Juliet Lynd, who has done invaluable critical and archival work on Vicuña's oeuvre, writes about this in her introduction to *El Zen Surado,* a poetry collection published in Chile by Editorial Catalonia in 2013. This book, in addition to being dedicated to *"the [female] students who march naked or dressed for the sake of justice. Poetry and the future depends on them,"* is also dedicated to Juliet Lynd, who "found these poems at the bottom of a drawer," a story that Vicuña has repeated to me: two thousand pages of writing from the late '60s found in the bottom of a trunk; it was work that for Vicuña was raw and meaningful and exciting.

Of Vicuña's contributions to the "artistic, political and cultural revolution" of Chile in the late '60s and early '70s, Lynd writes:

> Cecilia Vicuña was on the vanguard of this cultural scene: she lived in the margins, but her work (visual, performative and also poetic) of that era anticipated the important artistic and academic movements in conceptual art and performance that took off in the '70s and '80s, encapsulating even the discourses of second wave feminism. . . . Lucy Lippard has classified her small sculptures made from objects found on the beach in Concón in 1966 as a precursor by six months to Robert Smithson's Earthworks in the U.S.; they also predate the silhouettes of Ana Mendieta, the exiled Cuban artist who sketched feminine figures into the landscape in the '70s as well as the earth-drawings made by Atsuko Tanaka in Japan in 1968. Nemesio Antúnez, in response to "Otoño" in the Museum of Bellas Artes (in Santiago) in 1971 . . . informed Vicuña that she was making "conceptual art."

This was the first time Vicuña had heard the term "conceptual art," yet in her journal notes about the installation of "Autumn," she analyzes the piece as if she were an experienced practitioner. She writes that "Autumn" is "an interior piece rather than exterior one, because its conception and the experience of doing it counts more than the sculpture itself."

It's not an exaggeration to say that Cecilia Vicuña, at the age of 24, and without even meaning to be, was way ahead of her time as a maker of conceptual art in Chile. It is also not an exaggeration to emphasize that as a performance artist, as a feminist artist, as a visual artist, and as a literary artist, she was way ahead of her time not just in Chile, but around the world as well.

2

To return to her September 2015 performance at the Poetry Foundation in Chicago: I want to focus on a moment that took place during the after-talk when Vicuña was asked a question about translation.

The question energized her. She said:

Meeting the translators has been one of the most beautiful things that has ever happened to me. Because at the same time I arrived in the U.S. and wanted ... because I was expelled from the universe I was born into by the military coup in Chile ... and so when you are an expelled person, I think expelled is better than exiled because you are really nothing. You are, how do you call the little pulgas, you are like the fleas ... Chile and Latin America were really like a wet dog (she growls) ... and so I landed here as really an unwanted being, and soon enough I encountered the translators, and the translators are the opposite of that, the translators are the ones who want to open what nobody wants to see. And so the role of the translator is of an infinite importance, and that's one of the reasons why in American culture translators are so looked down upon, because they are building a sort of bridge to other imaginations and that is really the subversive act, to be able to see the thoughts, feelings, the darkness of others, but the darkness within, not the darkness that is perceived as a threat, the darkness that is like a pole attracting you. ... For example when I was reading about these monkey people (the Homo naledi—recently discovered in South Africa), our ancestors, I keep calling them monkey people because they are so beautiful, I don't know if you've seen the pictures, they look so intense, so human and yet they are totally hairy and well so, I think of them. ... I forgot what I was going to say because I was so caught up by the idea of the face of these creatures ('translation,' an audience member screams out). ... Translation—it's the darkness. The way this cave was discovered was very unusual. There was a tiny woman archaeologist who dared go through a crack so small. It was really child size and these ancient monkeys found this cave and entered purposefully time and time again to perform a ritual. And one of the things the article says is that animals don't go into the dark, animals don't like the dark, so that implies that probably they already had fire, we don't know that yet, I haven't yet encountered that information, but the fact that they were going into the dark means for me the opposite: why were they already looking for the dark two million years ago? It's because in that darkness, which for me represents translation ... when Rosa (Alcalá) goes into the poem, she sees in the poem what not even I saw, she sees what the poem itself saw. And that is the value of translation ...

An introductory note like this one does not usually spend too much time acknowledging the work of translators. But I want to take my cue from Vicuña here, and to make a special note of just how remarkable the translations in this book are, and to offer a cry of gratitude from outside of the cave to those great translators who entered the darkness, and who kept going back into the darkness, in order to help us have this collection: Rosa Alcalá, Esther Allen, Suzanne Jill Levine, Edwin Morgan, Urayoán Noel, James O'Hern, Anne Twitty, Eliot Weinberger, and Christopher Winks. And with special thanks for the amazing editorial work that Rosa Alcalá has done in putting together this collection, and in putting together previous collections, including *Spit Temple: The Selected Performances of Cecilia Vicuña* (2012).

For seeing in the poems even more than what Vicuña saw: thank you, Rosa, and thanks to all the translators: muchísimas, muchísimas gracias!

And I want, as well, to focus for a moment on the movements and connections Vicuña makes in her answer to this question. I am specifically interested in the primal and prophetic role she ascribes to translation: the strange compulsion translators feel to enter the darkness in order to show us more than what we can see on our own. In her answer, Vicuña posits the idea that translation has a special role to play in providing an identity for dissident writers, for exiled writers, for expelled writers, for writers who, in her terms, nobody wants to see. This is consistent with something Vicuña has said to me in conversation about how she has been viewed in Chile throughout her career. In her words, in Chile she has until recently mostly been ignored. But through translation, she tells us, she was able to be seen outside of Chile, and outside the confines of a nationalism that sought to expel her. Translation, then, we might say, serves as a means of exploding the imaginary yet powerfully prohibitive borders imposed by nationalism. It exposes the illusory nature of those borders, and can make us all aware of how damaging they can actually be. Interestingly, Vicuña's forthcoming book, *El Poema Animal/La Danza del Venado* (Hueders, 2016, Chile), a work kept hidden until now, is, she has told me, a translation and a meditation on the art of translation.

Dictatorships violently clarify ambiguities. As an exile, as a feminist, as a person who lost friends and family members to the military dictatorship, as a person who lost her country because of the military dictatorship, as someone who has always acknowledged and vehemently supported the dissemination of indigenous art, as an observer of U.S. culture, as someone out of place in two countries—Chile and the U.S., where she has lived for over 30 years—and as a member of no nation, Vicuña has always constructed her work from a position of resistance: to fascist government, to social hierarchies, to corporate power structures, to sexist power structures, to good taste, to the fashions of even the experimental art world. She is a poet, a performer, a visual artist, an anthologist, and, among other things, a radical archivist. In the process, though, she is a model of how one lives her life in the struggles of art and politics through presence, through resilience, through continuous innovation, through a relentless questioning of history and tradition, through an idealism that is not naive, an idealism that understands how bad the world is, an idealism which believes that we need art to report the horrors, to explain the horrors, to critique the horrors; we need art about the horrors to make our own horrible lives a little bit more worth living.

3

As I mentioned before, in conversation Vicuña has repeatedly stated that throughout her career she has not been as respected inside of Chile as she has been on the outside. If this is indeed the case, then we can speculate on a number of causes.

The first gets us right into the context in which the opening poems in this book were produced. In addition to a ferocious sense of experimentation, Vicuña's early work is fueled by idealism, excitement, and a desire to support and participate in Chile's democratically forged socialist revolution, as in this writing from *Saborami*, from a page that is dated August 22, 1973, just a few weeks before September 11, when General Pinochet's military coup overthrew Salvador Allende and his Popular Unity government. She writes:

> Latin America should never become like Europe or the U.S. . . . Chile could be the first happy country in the world, a way of being constantly affectionate would grow from innocence and neolithic ecstasy. Suicide wouldn't exist. Socialism would achieve a cosmic consciousness, the sum of the wisdom of the pre-Columbian Indians and of the many wisdoms of other places. Socialism in Latin America would give birth to a culture in which "thinking with the belly" would reveal so much more than "thinking with the head." Thought, perception would grow with increasing joy. There would be much dancing, much music, much friendship. Socialism in Chile could give birth to a joyful way of living.

So, on the one hand, we see Vicuña dreaming of a utopia, a hope that the good she saw in Salvador Allende's egalitarianism, in his focus on educating and medically caring for the poorest of the poor, would "give birth to a joyful way of living."

But, on the other hand, Vicuña's feminism and, in a different way, her eroticism, was neither understood nor cared for by the radical left. It's safe to say, I think, that when she spoke of the political and economic realities of the nation, she was accepted by the power brokers of the left. But when her work turned more personal, when her work turned toward the erotics of the body, the leftist men controlling the discourse didn't quite know what to make of her.

Which is to say that from the time Vicuña left Chile in 1972, before the coup, her authenticity as a Chilean, as a member of the nation, as she who has the ability to speak authoritatively about what it means to be a Chilean, had already been called into question. Vicuña's aesthetic radicalism and feminist positioning was beyond the imagination of socialist Chile in 1972 and continues to be beyond the imagination for many readers and critics today. We can say that she was not fully accepted by the political left during the brief tenure of the Popular Unity party in Chile. And while she has maintained a readership in Chile over the decades, it seems correct as well to say that for some she would continue to not be accepted as a writer with authentic dissident credentials.

This is complicated stuff and gets even more complicated by a rupture that formed between the dissident writers who stayed in Chile during the Pinochet dictatorship and the dissident writers who left. Roberto Bolaño's writings that have been read so widely in the past 15 years have exposed this divide by shedding light on the ways in which dissident solidarity (a shared identification with Chile's short-lived socialist project, as well as a shared sense of oppression and exclusion by the dictatorship and the new social order) can easily mutate into an exclusivist form of reverse-nationalism (the leftists inside the country telling the leftists outside the country that they have lost their legitimacy to speak authoritatively about the nation) that contributes to the nullification of the exile. For, as Bolaño and Vicuña might tell it, a certain breed of writer and artist who stayed in Chile questioned the legitimacy of the critiques levied by a certain breed of writer and artist who left (and as Bolaño has made clear, the opposite is also true). The legitimacy of the exiles' critiques was questioned because of the location of the body of the writer. More generously, perhaps, is the generalized idea that the writers who stayed had to suffer in ways that the writers who left could not imagine (and again, these are complicated, impossible questions). I don't want to spend too much time on these ruptures. To be honest, I don't truly understand them. Or, more accurately, I understand from my family experience the complications that follow the decision to leave or not return to an oppressive country, and I understand how truly awful it was for so many people who stayed or could not leave. And I understand the resentments that were felt for those who left, and I understand the ways in which families and friends inevitably grew apart and were broken through exile.

More to the point, I want to return to something I mentioned earlier: the dedication to the 2013 publication of *El Zen Surado*, which honors:

> the (female) students who march naked or dressed for the sake of justice. Poetry and the future depends on them.

In conversation, Vicuña has remarked that attitudes in Chile toward her work have changed in recent years. She attributes this change to the student movements that emerged in 2012 to protest the privatization of public education, and the exorbitant fees and loans facing college students and their families. Chile under Pinochet became the laboratory for the extreme neoliberal practices dreamed up by Milton Friedman and the economists known as the Chicago Boys. The privatization of public services, especially education, was at the heart of these plans that radically reshaped and diminished the government's role in providing for its citizenry. In this sense, the Chilean educational system, which has largely been privatized and corporatized, a system in which the majority of students don't attend public schools, and as a result they accumulate dramatic debt even before they enter university, has paved the way for the reshaping of public education policies in the U.S. Moreover, Chile ranks second to the U.S. as the most expensive university system in the world. For-profit universities, high interest rates on student loans, and a system in which the government barely contributes to the cost of higher education have resulted in large quantities of families going broke and students not finishing their studies.

In 2012 this was nothing new. The country was in its fourth decade of such policies. However, what was new in 2012 was the attitude of the young people who were affected by these policies. And these young people have recently embraced Vicuña by publishing her books, curating gallery shows for her, and inviting her to speak and perform.

The dictatorship lasted from 1973 to 1990. By 2012 the country had been in the post-dictatorship era for a longer period of time than the dictatorship had lasted. However, the dictatorship is still present. As the education system demonstrates, the economic and social policies birthed in the dictatorship still hold sway. What's more difficult to see from the outside, though, is just how hard it has been for Chileans in the post-dictatorship era to feel safe enough to protest, to feel free enough to speak the truth about the ugly policies of their current government. The students in 2012 were widely recognized as launching the first large-scale protests since the fall of the dictatorship. And this generation, which came of age in the post-dictatorship era, has been able to articulate a cogent and poignant critique of contemporary Chile that rejects the belief that the dictatorship had a clear end date. The dictatorship still exists for these students, and they have demonstrated publicly and loudly, providing the country with a vibrant and angry critique, a public rage that has not been voiced since the protest movements of the 1980s. And it is in this context that Vicuña's work in Chile is finally beginning to resonate.

Writing in *The Huffington Post*, NYU Professor of Education Gary Anderson illustrates the joyful, adventurous, and almost utopian spirit embodied by the 2012 protesters.

"Chilean students," he writes, "are experimenting with new forms of protest, such as marathon runs around congress, kiss-ins, and a 3,000-student performance of Michael Jackson's 'Thriller' to imply that the education system in Chile has become a zombie."

Kiss-ins, or *besatones*, are events in which thousands of young people gather in the streets and in plazas to make out as a jubilant act of protest. One wonders if the spirit found in Vicuña's poem "Research Project," from 1971, had given them their inspiration:

THE KISSERS we'll kiss

every person

we meet

to determine

who does it better

and learn accordingly

from their technique,

we'll practice it

and without delay bring it back

to our socialist country,

which will be land of The Kissers.

4

The Tribu No (The No Tribe) was an informal group of poets and artists who created art actions in Santiago, Chile, from 1967 to 1972. Vicuña founded and named the group and authored its manifesto, which states:

we manifest no desire and no characteristic. to avoid being pigeonholed we put forth no manifesto. and we are not worried we'll pigeonhole ourselves. that would be as likely as suddenly becoming polynesia's most daring parachutists.

(...)

we hope to turn solitude into the world's new idol.

ha ha

we say no-thing. after speaking centuries of IT, IT remains a secret.

our macabre intent is to leave humans naked, without preconceived notions, without conventional attachments-attire.

have no fear. our works will take years to manifest. we are not playing around. the interior of the seed is soft.

IT is known only by living IT. whatever IT is.

IT is yet to be discovered.

(*No Manifesto of The No Tribe*)

According to art critic M. Catherine de Zegher, the Tribu No "issued manifestos and staged public interventions," and it reflected Vicuña's belief that "the only contributions of the inhabitants of the Southern Hemisphere in the second part of the twentieth century was to say no." As de Zegher writes, among their many interventions are the creation of "a dictionary of sexist words and insults, and an encyclopedia of disgust."

Vicuña recently told me that there is also a renewed interest in the Tribu No in Chile among the same group of young writers and artists who have recently begun to promote her poetry, performance art, and visual art. And, in fact, the aforementioned Juliet Lynd wrote a book about the Tribu No, published in Chile in 2016, including documents and photos of the early performances created by Vicuña with the collective. To take this a bit further, there is a renewed interest in saying "No," and in the idea that saying "No" is the most important contribution we can make as we participate in certain forms of social discourse. It's a "No" voiced to the powers that be, but it's a different kind of "No" as well. It's a tactical "No," a refusal to explain or justify positions, actions, and beliefs in order to comfort those who might not understand.

Again, returning to the ways in which Vicuña's work has been globally ahead of its time, I want to point to the Winter 2015 issue of the *Chicago Review*, which includes a folio on "Sexism and Sexual Assault in Literary Communities." And within the folio is a collectively and anonymously authored piece called the "No Manifesto for Poetry Readings and LISTSERVs and Magazines and 'Open Versatile Spaces Where Cultural Production Flourishes.'" The manifesto is written "after Yvonne Rainer," the dancer whose "No Manifesto" of 1965 elucidates positions that are both aesthetic and political, and which contextualizes the relationship between audience and performer:

NO to spectacle

No to virtuosity

No to transformations and magic and make-believe

No to the glamour and transcendence of the star image

No to the heroic no to the anti-heroic

No to trash imagery no to involvement of performer or spectator

No to style

No to camp

No to seduction of spectator by the wiles of the performer

No to eccentricity

No to moving or being moved

I recently emailed Vicuña to ask if in 1967 in Chile she had read Rainer's "No Manifesto" from 1965. She said:

> I didn't know anything about Yvonne Rainer's "No Manifesto" until this very moment. I just Googled it, and I think the relationship between the two texts is fantastic. It's impossible that I would have known about her in Chile in 1967. But undoubtedly those ideas were in the air.

Writing in 1967, Vicuña offers her own kind of "No Manifesto," which, among other things, accurately foretells her own continued refusal to be pigeonholed and to pigeonhole herself. As Juliet Lynd writes, "With the 'No Manifesto,' Vicuña suggests that the interventions of the Tribu No are gestures whose effect is yet to be determined; they are created in the service of vital social transformation, and not for the acquisition of political power."

In 2015 we get yet another "No Manifesto," which in several pages elucidates the many violent dangers that any poet who is not a cisgender man confronts in U.S. poetry communities. In their "No Manifesto," the collective offers not a solution, but a way of speaking back to power, by articulating "No" to as many predators and predatory scenarios that might possibly be faced.

No to using the concept of solidarity as a way to shame other women

No to calling men by their last names and women by their first names in reviews, talks, and introductions

No to introducing someone at poetry readings with sexualized references to their appearance, clothing choices, or body parts

No to introducing someone at poetry readings with emphasized or judgmental references to their age

No to introducing someone at poetry readings with references to how much of an influence you or seminal male poets have had on their work

No to suggesting students of seminal male poets would be nothing without them

No to thinking "we" can speak as one and no to assuming "we" know what "you" think

There is much to say about this most recent "No Manifesto," though this isn't the appropriate venue to do so. The point I wish to emphasize, however, is the way in which Vicuña's work from the 1960s and '70s, in general, and the "No Manifesto of The No Tribe" in particular, seems utterly relevant at this particular moment in our social and literary environments. "NO" is a refusal that's applicable in a multitude of ages, contexts, and cultures. This "NO," this refusal, is a political and social strategy that was relevant in 1967, is relevant in 2017, and will continue to be relevant for decades to come. For Vicuña, in Chile in 1967, there was a singular urgency to the fight she was waging against sexism and misogyny, and in a context that was not at all receptive to its convictions. That urgency is still alive in the struggles being waged today.

5

This book, with its Precarios, its Stupid Diary entries, its QUIPOems, its drawings, its hexagons, its translations, its multilingual sound pieces, its narrative performance texts, its manifestos: it's as unpigeonholable as Vicuña has been throughout the 50 years she has been making our world better by making her amazing and irrepressible art. This book is long overdue, or it has come at absolutely the right time. For in Vicuña we have an artist who is always working her way through the impossible, through the unspeakable, and through the voices that do not get absorbed.

Of the many emotional responses that Vicuña's work inspires in me, the one that stands out to me the most is the feeling of being haunted by the many ways in which the bodies around us are beaten, forgotten, or disappeared.

"The dream of social justice pervades the history of Chile and Latin America," writes Vicuña in her afterword to the 2011 reproduction of *Saborami*, which she dedicates to the memory of her uncle Carlos Enrique, who was disappeared by the dictatorship. "It began in ancient times and continues today. It never dies yet is always thwarted. *Saborami* is the broken heart of an era. A heart dropped into the sea with the bodies of the disappeared."

And the dream of social justice, as we see in Vicuña's more recent work, pervades her view of what is possible in the U.S. as well.

I am haunted, specifically, by the story Vicuña tells in the performance she gave at Woodland Pattern Book Center in Milwaukee on September 29, 2001, a few weeks after September 11, of a disappeared man named Luis, an Ecuadorian migrant to New York, who was "digging a hole for Con Edison." In short, Luis falls asleep in the hole; his coworkers cover him with rubble and he dies:

> And his brother
> came to the work place and said:

Where is my brother Luis?

Your brother Luis? Nobody even remembered him

And this is very telling

because this is like our position

the position of the little dark ones

Nobody even notices

whether we are

or we are not

there

And this man, the brother,

insisted: He's here in this hole (tapping lectern)

And they fought him and said no, no he's not

He probably disappeared

He went somewhere else

If he was here we don't remember

Denying the whole thing

Until he pressed, he pressed, he pressed, and finally they opened the hole and there it was:

Luis, crushed, like this

Of course, he was dead

So this poem is in memory of Luis Gómez

I want to conclude for a moment by thinking about the specificity of this story, Vicuña's insistence on naming Luis Gómez, and the act of dedicating her work to his memory.

The great Chilean poet Raúl Zurita has stated in conversation with me that one goal of his poetry is to keep those Chileans who disappeared during the dictatorship from disappearing again and again. This, of course, is, on one level, an impossible hope, an impossible task that can only end with a failure. But on another level, for Zurita, for Vicuña, poetry—and this we see in the story of Luis Gómez—creates a public record. It gives the dead—it gives Luis Gómez—more respect than he was given by the state, by his employers and colleagues, and by the neoliberal forces responsible for the oppressive conditions of where he was born, the oppressive conditions he experienced throughout his migration, and the oppressive conditions that allowed for his unnoticed death and disappearance. To return to Vicuña's earlier discussion of translation: here is work that takes us into the darkness to help us see more than we would be able to otherwise see about that which is taking place before our very own eyes. The holes in which immigrants are literally dying. The unnoticed sounds of their deaths.

I want to thank Vicuña for keeping these memories alive, for inviting us to mourn with her, and for helping us to see our own responsibilities to keep those who have died brutally and needlessly from disappearing again, and to do all that we can to make visible that which we do not want to see.

Note on the Translations

Unless indicated by initials, all translations are by Rosa Alcalá, or written/performed originally in English by Cecilia Vicuña.

Key to the initials

EA	Esther Allen
SJL	Suzanne Jill Levine
EM	Edwin Morgan
UN	Urayoán Noel
JOH	James O'Hern
AT	Anne Twitty
EW	Eliot Weinberger
CW	Christopher Winks
CV	Cecilia Vicuña

Trailed out, this fluttering, thread of life:

no use saying it's tethered to the very
source of earth's life-bringing change.

—Meng Chiao

(translated by David Hinton)

new
and

selected poems

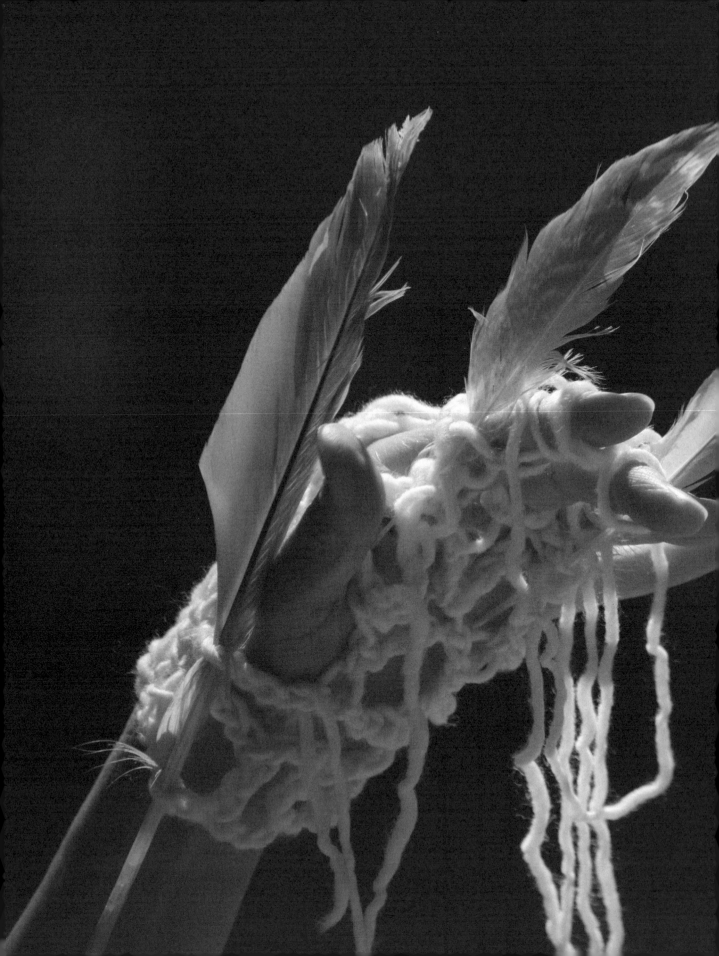

The selvedge of the book receives the hand.

A limit is a limen, a door to go through.

The border asks, can we go beyond our self's edge?

The self of a culture now destroying the earth?

Let the hand respond, her sweat knows.

.

Book's Breath (Poetics)

In the book's darkness, gold shines.

Not a fire's light, but an interior illumination, say the Kogi: When vision is lost a dance in the dark commences, "to a barely audible song." —Gerardo Reichel-Dolmatoff

Writing is darkness.

The body of experience.

"What is hidden completes us," says Lezama Lima:

"When an ominous cloud looms over the world, I stubbornly take refuge in that which is furthest from us." —Lezama Lima, quoting Goëthe

"Knowledge not ours and what we don't know form true wisdom […] in the fullness of breath is a universal rhythm, a breath that joins the visible to the invisible."

"In this way I found in each word a seed sprouted from the union of the stellar and the visceral."
    —José Lezama Lima, *Las eras imaginarias*

"Grinning wildly he (she)
drinks the blood and guts
of demons turned into elixir"
    —The Mahakala Panjaranatha, from *Wisdom and Compassion:
    The Sacred Art of Tibet*, by Marylin M. Rhie and Robert A.F. Thurman

"The Mahakala, the Black One, the fierce protector of the Dharma … reflects the void, the truth body." (Ibid.)

El polvo rojo de la actividad iluminada.

El vacío exige un retorno a la interdependencia radical de todas las cosas,
obras realizadas fuera del espacio y el tiempo.

Poetry is a supreme affinity with the world's speech.
Speech meaning a secret breath.
Inhalation and exhalation, the world's heart beating
in a common language of perception.

To hear in the interior of a word what is not word keeps its engine going.

NEW YORK, AUGUST 2015

Stupid Diary

AUTHOR'S NOTE: The *Sabor a Mí* (*Taste of Me*) poems are an extract of *The Stupid Diary*, an unpublished manuscript of more than 2,000 pages, written in Santiago de Chile during the height of the movement that led to Salvador Allende's presidential election in 1970. Some of the poems in *The Stupid Diary* became part of the first *Sabor a Mí* of 1971, which, despite a signed contract with Ediciones Universitarias de la Universidad Católica de Valparaíso (UCV), was never published. The second *Saborami,* published in England by Beau Geste Press in 1973, included 20 poems from *The Stupid Diary*, and, in 2013, 100 poems from the manuscript were published in Chile as *El Zen Surado* by Editorial Catalonia. Juliet Lynd, in her introduction to *El Zen Surado*, cites testimony that offers two possible reasons the first *Sabor a Mí* was never published: either it was censored before the Chilean coup of September 11, 1973, or the military threw it into the ocean, along with other books, after the coup.

Saborami, Beau Geste Press (Devon, England, 1973).

El Zen Surado, Editorial Catalonia (Chile, 2013).

~ ~

NOTA DE LA AUTORA: Los poemas de *Sabor a Mí* son un extracto del *Diario Estúpido*, un manuscrito de 2,000 páginas que permanece inédito, escrito en Santiago de Chile durante el período álgido del movimiento que llevó a Salvador Allende a la presidencia en 1970. Algunos poemas del *Diario Estúpido* conformaron el primer *Sabor a Mí* de 1971, un manuscrito que no se publicó a pesar de haber firmado contrato de publicación con Ediciones Universitarias de la Universidad Católica de Valparaíso (UCV). Un testimonio recogido por Juliet Lynd indica que *Sabor a Mí* o fue censurado, o fue lanzado al mar, junto a otros libros, por los militares después del golpe militar del 11 de Septiembre de 1973. El segundo *Saborami*, publicado en Inglaterra por Beau Geste Press en 1973, incluía 20 poemas del *Diario Estúpido*. En el 2013, 100 poemas del *Diario Estúpido* se publicaron en Chile en *El Zen Surado*, Catalonia.

Para seguir construyendo el socia   lismo en chile
necesitamos un milagro: que se desin
tegre la CIA, que los militares   no den un
golpe de estado, que se pudra   la demo
cracia cristiana, que se mueran   los momios.

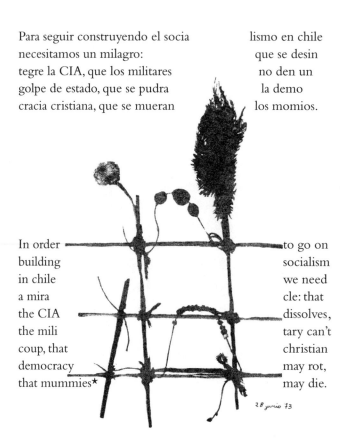

In order   to go on
building   socialism
in chile   we need
a mira   cle: that
the CIA   that dissolves,
the mili   tary can't
coup, that   christian
democracy   may rot,
that mummies★   may die.

28 junio 73

★mummy is a reactionary person.

La violencia
revolucionaria
es como
un clavo
martillado
en una hoja
de plátano
oriental:
un
movimiento
brusco
captura
lo delicado,
un haiku
o
un salto
de Tai chi.

31 julio 73

Revolutionary
violence
is a nail
hammered
on a
banana leaf.
A rough
movement
to capture
the delicate,
an haiku
or a leap
of Tai chi.

Clepsidra

Antiguamente bordé sobre mi cabeza
las marcas del abandono y el fracaso
nadie tenía la fortuna de saber
a qué galaxias aludo
con mi sonrisa.
Opté por los senderitos salvajes,
el objeto de la poesía
siempre fue crear
rondas colectivas y espirituales
donde las cábalas
Juno y Aristóteles
bailan entre arbustos nuevos.
Desde el primer momento
conté con mi estupidez
y mi falta general de talento.
Siempre naufragué entre
sustantivos y verbos.
Me sentía y me siento
un predicador del asco:
a nadie ilumino
más que a mí.

1966

Clepsydra

I embroidered on my head long ago
the signs of abandonment and failure
no one had the fortune of knowing
to which galaxies I allude
with my smile.
I opted for wild trails,
the object of poetry
was always to create
spiritual and collective rings
where conjecture,
Juno, and Aristotle
dance among new shrubs.
From the beginning
I relied on my stupidity
and general lack of talent.
Always I shipwrecked among
nouns and verbs.
I continue to feel I am
a shitty preacher:
I enlighten no one
more than me.

1966

Teresa la Imbécil

Mis amores en realidad
son la caja extraña de una muñeca polaca
Los ojos de la rubia apareciendo
sobre las caderas mucho después de la medianoche
la buhardilla siempre está especial
para soltar el enorme cabello
en la espalda y caen las hebras finas y gruesas
por su mentón de nutria
Deliberadamente asomaba su rostro en la pared
y no se veía más que la sombra de los senos
ocultos bajo marmotas de pelo
Y tan encantador el resplandor de su piel
a esa hora desusada
Los desvíos de la cintura
se distinguían claramente
como abejas en el césped
la ventana no estaba abierta ni cerrada
lo que yo veía, amarillo como cristal
se desprendía de las caderas soñolientas
amasadas en torniquetes impropios
Todo lo que yo veía era un destello pálido
de los pelos que se abren delicadamente
y dejan ver la piel rosada o verde ya no lo sé
de las caderas a un millón de centímetros
de mis miradas.

1968

Teresa the Idiot

In reality my loves
are the strange box of a Polish doll
The blonde's eyes appearing
fixed to her hips long after midnight
the garret always singular to loosen
a massive mane
across her back, its strands
thick and fine draping
her otter-like chin
Deliberately she'd peer out from the wall
and nothing could be seen but the shadow of her breasts
hidden beneath marmots of hair
And lovely was her skin's radiance
at that unusual hour
Her waist's digressions
easily discerned
as bees through grass
the window neither open nor closed
What I saw, yellow like crystal,
rose from sleepy thighs
amassed in unseemly tourniquets
Everything before me, a pale shimmer
of hairs fanning delicately
to reveal the pink or green skin I no longer know
of hips a million centimeters
from my gaze.

1968

Misión

Te propongo hacer un viaje
alrededor del mundo,
acreditados como:
                "Misión investigadora
                del gobierno socialista".
Tú y yo seremos
los "besadores".
Besamos mejor que nadie
habiendo desarrollado
una técnica minuciosa
y altamente estudiada
de cómo besar más perfectamente.
No hay mujer que bese como yo
ni hombre que bese como tú.

LOS BESADORES besaremos
a todas las personas
que encontremos,
para descubrir
quien sabe hacerlo mejor
y aprender por tanto
su técnica,
para practicarla
y enseguida traerla
a nuestro país socialista,
que será el país de Los Besadores.

ABRIL 1971

Research Project

I propose we take a trip
around the world,
to be officially designated:

<blockquote>
"Socialist government
research project."
</blockquote>

You and I will be
the "kissers."
We kiss better than anyone,
having developed
a meticulous
and carefully researched
method for perfecting the kiss.
There is no woman who kisses like me
and no man who kisses like you.

THE KISSERS we'll kiss
every person
we meet
to determine
who does it better
and learn accordingly
from their technique,
we'll practice it
and without delay bring it back
to our socialist country,
which will be land of The Kissers.

APRIL 1971

La Gitana Dormida
(Un león vigila su
cuaderno de sueños)

La Gitana ha escrito durante años
una obra secreta que nadie jamás
conocerá, pero que ha empezado
a realizarse en la vida real.

Mientras ella continúa soñando
sus sueños forman el mundo.

El león, sin embargo,
no puede dormir.
Si deja de vigilarla,
ella podría despertar
y nosotros desaparecer
instantáneamente.

The Sleeping Gypsy (A Lion Guards Her Dream Journal)

The Gypsy has been writing for many years
a secret text no one will ever
read, but which has begun
to materialize in real life.

While she continues dreaming
her dreams create the world.

The lion, however,
cannot sleep.
If he ceases to watch her,
she could awaken
and we vanish
instantly.

Voy al Encuentro

Voy al encuentro del milagro,
a nada más

Los sexos se iluminan
con el fulgor del deseo

Me vuelvo fosforescente
y le enseño el camino a la luna

Ella causa la menstruación
o los ovarios la hacen girar
cada 28 días?

I'm Off to Meet

I'm off to meet a miracle,
nothing more

In the brilliance of desire
your sex and mine are illuminated

I become phosphorescent
and show the moon the way

Does she bring on menstruation
or do the ovaries cause her to rotate
every 28 days?

Ruidos Desagradables

tic tac

ametralladora

explosión nuclear

discurso

bendición del papa

dictado de misa

enseñanza primaria secundaria general

declaración de guerra

ruido de dinero

chasquido de palmadas

rumor derechista

sedición

tijera que corta pelo

policía que viene

persona que obliga

Ruidos Agradables

asaltos de bancos

pis que cae

tam tam

ronquido

ronroneo

Unpleasant Noises

tick tock

machine gun

nuclear explosion

discourse

the pope's blessing

sermon

primary secondary general education

declaration of war

noise of money

the thwack of a spanking

right-wing buzz

sedition

scissors snipping hair

cops coming

a person coercing

Pleasant Noises

bank robberies

pee falling

tom tom

snore

purr

silencio

silencio

viento

lapicito pastel

pincelito

pasto que crece

susurros

ruidos de copulación

besos

chasquidos de cariños

pasos

nubes

truenos

lluvia

sol

risas

y

punes

FEBRERO 1968

silence
silence
wind
little pastel pencil
little paint brush
grass growing
whispers
copulatory noises
kisses
the thwack of a caress
footfalls
clouds
thunder
rain
sun
laughter
and
farts

FEBRUARY 1968

Horticultura

Durante épocas enteras

me cultivé a mí misma

como un demonio sin freno

y hoy me veo

con freno de mano

como niña de mano

deforme y delgada

en un jardín

de plantas de humo.

MARZO 1972

Horticulture

For ages
I cultivated myself
as a freewheeling devil
and now here I am
a handmaiden
with a handbrake
diminished and deformed
in a garden
filled with plants of smoke.

MARCH 1972

Cecilia Vicuña Ramírez
Lagarrigue etc.

Cecilia del latín
"la que no ve"
Vicuña del euskara
"tierra baja"
Lagarrigue de la garriga
"formación vegetal"
del vasco francés
y Ramírez
patronímico de antiguo
hijo de Ramiro
Mezcla de reyes con idiotas
hidalguía y vulgo
mierda y barro.

JUNIO 1971

Cecilia Vicuña Ramírez
Lagarrigue etc.

Cecilia from the Latin
"she who cannot see"
Vicuña from the Euskara
"lowland"
Lagarrigue from garrigue
"vegetal formation"
from the French Basque
and Ramírez
ancient patronym
son of Ramiro
Mixture of kings and idiots
nobility and commoner
shit and mud.

JUNE 1971

Lo Casual

La idea de encontrar lo casual como algo
que estaba cuidadosamente preparado
por una mano anterior que encadenó
sus formas estéticamente
para explicar un jardín desordenado
que está en el punto preciso de su desorden,
un gesto sin consumar, que se agita levemente
sin que se sepa qué va a ser de él.

La indeterminación, la musicalidad
del movimiento de algunas hierbas
abandonadas a sí mismas
doradas de sequedad
a causa de una emoción
que sufrió su dueña
que antes se ocupaba
tan tiernamente del alelí
y ahora ha dejado
que todo crezca
y solo visita el jardín
para dejarlo languidecer.
Azaroso y muelle
todo se ha cansado
y vive por casualidad.

29 AGOSTO 1970

Chance Encounter

The idea of coming upon the unexpected
as something carefully arranged
by a prior hand that linked
all its forms aesthetically
to explain a disordered garden
at the height of its disorder,
a gesture not yet carried out, gently stirring
with no way of knowing what will become of it.

Indeterminacy, the musical
sway of certain grasses
left to fend for themselves
brown and parched
consequence of an emotion
the owner suffered
she who so lovingly tended
to the wallflowers
and now has let them
grow wild
who visits the garden
only to let it languish.
Precarious, given to its fate,
all has become weary
and by chance lives.

29 AUGUST 1970

La Compañía de los Sueños
(Aviso económico)

La compañía tiene por objeto realizar
los sueños nocturnos del cliente:
                    Si usted
tiene un sueño, escribe a la compañía
que se encargará de reunir a todos
los personajes del sueño en el
ambiente natural del sueño.

La compañía no garantiza
la total realización del sueño.
El azar no depende
de ninguna compañía.
La compañía no falseará los sentimientos
de ningún personaje
por medio de la instrucción.

Si usted ha soñado que es besado
por un antiguo amante
en la cumbre de la montaña,
la compañía devolverá a su amante
a la cumbre de la montaña,
pero usted, ¿será besado?

1970

The Dream Company
(Classified Ad)

The company's objective is to fulfill
nocturnal dreams for its client:
                                        If you
have a dream, write to the company,
who will see to it
that all the characters in your dream
be gathered in a natural dream environment.

The company cannot guarantee
total realization of the dream.
Chance does not answer
to a company.
The company will not re-educate
any character
to falsify emotion.

If in a dream you were kissed
by an old lover
on a mountaintop,
the company will place your lover
on that mountaintop once again,
but you, will you be kissed?

1970

Nuevos Diseños Eróticos para Muebles

Soñando con un mundo vasto
hemos llegado a la certera conclusión
de que las posiciones del cuerpo
en el mundo civilizado
son demasiado limitadas
de modo que terminaremos
con la posición
    "sentada en una silla"
para proponer distintos muebles
que ofrezcan multiplicidad
de movimientos o situaciones corporales
a la conductora de sus propias carnes.

Esta idea será de fundamental interés
para las personas obsesionadas
u obligadas a permanecer
durante largo tiempo inmóviles
como son:
    estudiantes
    oficinistas
    operadores de fábricas
    asistentes a reuniones

Se crearán modelos para personas
que odien escribir sentadas

New Erotic Designs
for Furniture

Dreaming of a vast world
we have come to the definite conclusion
that physical positions
in a civilized world
are too constricting
therefore, we would eliminate
the position
      "sitting in a chair"
and suggest instead a different kind of furniture
that allows for a multiplicity
of movements and physical situations
in line with each body's specific wiring.

This idea will be of special interest
to those who obsessively
or by obligation remain
immobile for long hours,
e.g.:

      students
      office workers
      machine operators
      meeting attendees

Models will be built for those
who hate to write while sitting,

para que puedan hacerlo

hincadas, de boca, en cuclillas

o cabeza abajo

      Estos muebles irán

en beneficio de la salud

y la belleza de todos los interesados

gracias a la peculiar irrigación

sanguínea y la repentina

turgencia de muslos y nalgas

que sin duda tengo planeadas.

1971

allowing them to kneel,
lie on their bellies, squat,
or hang upside-down

                        This furniture will
promote the health
and beauty of all its users
thanks to the peculiar increase in blood circulation
and inevitable protuberance
of thighs and asses,
which are undoubtedly part of my plan.

1971

Luminosidad de los Orificios

Incluso puedo contarles algún cuento

hablarles de mi novio dulce ladrillo

de piel de origen indio y apariencia

volcánica con siete cráteres con

características propias

Uno por ejemplo tiene labios

y es el cráter de la paciencia

el más cómico y decidor

Además de él sale la poesía

encanto primordial de mi novio.

Hay dos cráteres en cambio de los que

no sale nada, sino que entran cosas

se llaman LAS ENTRADAS DE LA MÚSICA

y son algo rugosos

vulgarmente llamados orejas

son los aparatos más suaves del amor

los que mi novio no se lava por temor

a entorpecerlos o rayarlos

como quien destruye un disco

y con él se acaba una fuente de milagros.

Quedan otros 2 cráteres cuya función

es no solo dejar salir algo si no que

dejar entrar

Quedan sobre un órgano mojado

y hacen FUZ FUZ cuando funcionan

The Brilliance of Orifices

I can even tell you a story
talk about my boyfriend's
sweet brick skin, its Indian origin
and volcanic appearance
site of seven craters,
each with its own characteristics
One for example has lips
and is the patience crater
the funniest and most witty
It also releases poetry
my boyfriend's primary charm.
There are two craters however
through which things do not exit,
but enter
they are called ENTRANCES FOR MUSIC
and are somewhat wrinkled
crudely known as ears
they are the softest love devices
which my boyfriend never cleans
afraid he'll dull or scratch them
like someone who destroys a record
and with it a fount of miracles.
The function of the last two craters
is to allow things to exit
and also to enter
They cover a moist organ
and go FOOZ FOOZ when functioning

A ellos se debe la gracia del aroma
y la fetidez
Por éso se llaman despertadores
o INDICES DE LA SENSIBILIDAD
y al que se le desarrollan es un afortunado
y a mi novio le dicen LUCKY FORTUNATO
aunque se llama claudio.

FEBRERO 1968

To them we owe the grace of aroma
and funk
Which is why they are called awakeners
or INDEXES OF SENSITIVITY
and fortunate is he of the fully-developed awakeners
and they call my boyfriend LUCKY FORTUNATO
even though his name is claudio.

FEBRUARY 1968

Luxumei

Necesito decir
que mi atavío natural
son las flores
aunque me vestiré
de un modo increíble
con plumas
dientes de loco
y manojos de cabellera
de Taiwan y Luxumei.
Cada vez que estornudo
se llena el cielo de chispas
hago acrobacias
y piruetas endemoniadas
cada noche
me sale una espalda adyacente.
Soy de cuatro patas
preferentemente,
las ramas
me saldrán por la piel;
estoy obligada a ser
un ángel con la pelvis
en llamas.

Luxumei

To be clear
my natural attire
are flowers
though I dress
in a strange manner
with feathers
the teeth of crazy men
and handfuls of hair
from Taiwan and Luxumei.
Every time I sneeze
sparks fill the sky
I perform acrobatics
and diabolical pirouettes
every night
I grow an adjacent back.
I would prefer
to be on all fours,
branches
sprouting from my skin;
I am compelled to be
an angel with my pelvis
in flames.

Poema Puritano

Me encanta mi sexo
Entre tu sexo y el mío
no sé cuál elegir.

Es que el tuyo
es tan divertido
y el mío tan bonito.

Pero lo que hay
que subrayar
es como cabe el tuyo
dentro del mío
siendo tan grande
y de color brillante.

Los sexos son
en sí mismos
perfumados.

Morir con la mano en el sexo.

No con la mano en la mano,
aunque de eso puede encargarse
la otra mano.

Puritan Poem

I love my sex
Between your sex and my own
I don't know which to choose.

It's just that yours
is so much fun
and mine so pretty.

But what must
be highlighted
is how yours fits
inside of mine
when it is so big
and brilliant in color.

The sexes are
self-perfumed.

To die with a hand on one's sex.

Not hand in hand,
although that can be accomplished
by the other hand.

Amada Amiga

Las personas que me visitan
no imaginan
lo que desencadenan en mí.

C. no sabe que sueño
con mirarla sin que me vea.
Mientras le echa dulce de camote
al pan parece que juega
con cálices y piedras sagradas.
El modo como levanta la mano
para llenar el cuchillo
de mantequilla
es un gesto
donde los mares hacen equilibrio
donde las mujeres que tienen frío
se solazan.
Tiene oleajes y consecuencias
como una línea en el radar.
Cuando se levanta la falda
para mostrarme el calzón plateado
veo grupos ondulantes de caderas
que repiten la redondez
y la perfección
hasta alcanzar una estridencia
grande.

Beloved Friend

The people who visit me
can't imagine
what they unleash in me.

C. doesn't know that I dream
of looking at her without her seeing me.
While she spreads jam
on her bread she seems
to be playing with chalices and sacred stones.
The way she raises her hand
to fill the knife
with butter
is a gesture
where oceans balance,
where women who feel cold
find comfort,
whose waves and repercussions are
like a line on a radar screen.
When she raises her skirt
to show me her silvery panties
I see undulating hips
multiplying the roundness
to a noisy perfection.

Anhelo que no se mueva
para alcanzar a vivir en ella,
a respirar y dormir
en esas planicies.

Está tan oscuro el muslo
tan brillante el pelo
que parece habla en otro idioma.
Lo que digo es tan torpe
pero cómo voy a decir:

> "Eres tan hermosa"

> "Me alegro tanto
> de que hayas llegado."

Cuando subo el libro del Renacimiento
donde vemos primitivos italianos
quisiera decirte:

> "En esta ciudad te encuentro."

> "Tú eres esas colinas."

> "Tú las pintaste."

Tus dedos son iguales
a la curva de las aletas
de la sirena
representada en la alegoría.
Pero no es exactamente esto.
Tú eres un país con ciudades
de Lorenzetti
Tú y yo alguna vez
volveremos a esa ciudad.

No sufras porque en este cuadro
dos mujeres se acarician
yo alguna vez te acariciaré.
No te preocupes de que estés envejeciendo,

If only she'd not move
so that I could live in her,
breathe and sleep
upon those plains.

Her thigh is so dark,
hair so shiny
that it seems like speech in another language.
What I say is so clumsy
but how can I say:

       "You are so beautiful."

       "I am so happy

       you've come."

When I bring up the book of the Renaissance paintings
where we examine the Italian primitives
I would like to say:

       "I meet you in this city."

       "You are these hills."

       "You painted them."

Your fingers are identical
to the curving fins
of a siren in the allegory—
but that's not it.
You are a country
of Lorenzetti cities.
Sometime you and I
will return to that city.

Don't suffer because in this painting
two women caress each other.
Sometime I will caress you.
Don't worry because you're growing older

tú vas a otra clase de tiempo
y yo también.
Aliméntate del relato que me haces
de la copa de vino
cruzando el umbral.
Aliméntate y enjóyate,
no dejes de soñar con el cuadro
del maestro de Fontainebleau
donde una mujer
le toma a otra un pezón:
durante épocas enteras
nadie soltará tu pezón.

Quiero sufrir
enterrarme en ti
ahorcarte y hacer un hoyo profundo,
donde te empiece a tapar la tierra
lentamente y ver tus colores
podrirse bajo el café.
¿No te gusta tanto la combinación
de violeta y café?

No quería hablarte de la muerte
pero ya que la temes tanto
¿cómo no voy a hablar?
Es escaso el tiempo
que tenemos para vernos
y conversar.
Me gustaría ser hombre
para seducirte y obligarte
a que abandones tu casa
y te olvides de todo,
pero esta idea no me gusta.

You're moving on to another time
and me too.
Nourish yourself on the story you're telling
about the wine glass
crossing the threshold.
Nourish, enjoy yourself,
keep on dreaming about the painting
by the Fontainebleau master
in which one woman
tweaks another woman's nipple.
For centuries nobody
will let go of your nipple.

I want to suffer,
bury myself in you.
Strangle you and dig a deep hole
where the earth begins slowly
to cover you and I want to see your colors
begin to rot under the brown earth.
Don't you love the combination
of violet and brown?

I didn't mean to mention death,
but since you're so afraid,
how can I help it?
We don't have much time
to talk.
I wish I were a man
I'd seduce you and make
you leave home and forget
everything, but I don't like
that idea.

Separados y solitarios
los hombres siempre están fuera
y nada necesitan con más urgencia
que estar dentro,
probar alguna tibieza,
altas y bajasmar.

Estoy cansada de ti

Nunca te dejas llevar,
me gusta más que no lo hagas,
cuando lo haces
parece que el corazón te va a estallar
                              te va a florecer
                              te va a doler.

Es de mí que me canso.
Deseo verte nada más
que te enamores de otros
y nunca te apercibas de mí.

Cuando te vistes con camisa de franela
y calcetines de lana
por una semana
y te afeas y avejentas
para morir un poco
quiero estar cuando resucites
y seas una gloria de ojos húmedos
y oscuros.

Quiero ser un indio
que está escondido en las montañas
y nunca viene a las laderas
porque todo le duele.

Isolated, solitary, men are
always outside, needing
nothing more urgently
than to be inside,
to feel warmth,
the tidal flow.

I'm tired of you,
you never let yourself go.
It's better when you don't
when you do
it seems your heart will burst
                    will flower
                    will hurt.

It's me I'm tired of,
I want only to see you,
watch you fall in love with men
and never notice me.

After you've been wearing
a flannel shirt and wool socks
for a week,
making yourself old and ugly
to die a little,
I want to be there
when you come back to life
in a glory of moist
dark eyes.

I want to be an Indian
hiding in the hills
who never comes down the valleys
because everything hurts.

Iluminarme con mis propias luces.

Naciste del cruce
de tu madre con la muerte,
ni siquiera en la infancia
habrás sido rosada.
Los que hacen el amor contigo
creen que nunca regresarán
que se van a hundir
que les vas a tejer
una tela húmeda en la espalda y como es probable
que tengas conexiones
con la boca de los volcanes
por ahí tirarás a tus amantes
y si ellos se liberan es porque te compadeces.

Te tengo miedo
porque no puedes mirarme
como yo te miro
no puedes amarme
como te amo
no puedes ni siquiera
desear acariciarme
y vivir algún tiempo conmigo
haciéndome peinados góticos
o pidiéndome que revuelva el té
con la punta de mi pezón.

Tu lado humano
no está a la altura
de tu lado bestial.
Algunos te imaginan dueña
de regiones orgullosas

To be enlightened by my own lights.

You were born of the cross
between death and your mother.
Not even as a baby
could you have been rosy.
People who make love with you
think they'll never return,
they'll sink, you'll weave
a damp web to their shoulders
and, since you probably connect
with the mouths of volcanoes, there
you'll hurl your lovers
never to emerge
unless you take pity.

I'm afraid of you
because you can't look at me
as I look at you,
can't even want
to caress me
and live with me awhile,
doing my hair up in Gothic twists
or asking me to stir the tea
with the tip of my nipple.

Your human side is
not as fine
as your bestial nature.
Some think you reign
over proud,
menacing regions

y llenas de daño,

pero los que te han visto

con fiebre

o en épocas de menstruación

te aman muy en contra

de tu voluntad,

si es que tienes voluntad.

Solamente una intensidad

le da poderes a tu vida

y la muerte se ve acabada

por fuentes peludas

y calientes miradas.

Qué daría la muerte

porque no tuvieras

esos ojos redondos

ni esos senos

ni esos muslos

para dominarte

envolverte y guardarte

de una vez por todas.

JULIO 1970

but those who have seen you
feverish
or at menstrual times
love you against
your will.
If you have a will.
Only intensity
gives your life power
and death finds its undoing
in hairy fountains
and hot glances.

What wouldn't death give
to keep you from having
those round eyes
those breasts
those thighs
to master you
to wrap you up and
tuck you away forever.

JULY 1970

A.T.

Mondo

(Fragmentos del *Diario Estúpido*)

La poesía es una invitación de la irrealidad para que la realidad cambie de bando.

∎

El sexo es la mirada de dios.
La llave de la luz del día.

∎

¿Quién sabe de la luz?

El gran coito luminoso!

∎

Sufrimiento y felicidad son lo mismo para el alma que se ríe de todo.

En la luminosidad futura vamos a carecer de contingencia.

∎

El mar es el cielo de otro cielo.

∎

Mondo

(Excerpts from *The Stupid Diary*)

Poetry is the means by which unreality invites reality to switch sides.

▪

Sex is god's gaze.
Daylight's key.

▪

Who knows of light?

The great luminous coitus!

▪

Suffering and happiness are indistinguishable to the soul who laughs at it all.

In future luminosity we will lack contingency.

▪

The sea is the sky of another sky.

▪

Hay que traer al futuro e instalarlo entre los muslos como cosa ya hecha.

Vida instantánea y no mierda de vida.

■

El sexo es incorruptible.

■

Entre un hueco de muslo y una pizca de noche, Uxmal.

Marzo 1967

Dí de ellas

oh vagina negra
oh vagina roja
oh vagina de oro

piernas de marfil
              y no más!

Marzo 1967

■

Los pensamientos se digieren como un cereal, constituyen un alimento tan preciado como el natural.

Pueblos sin comida, pero con ideas han sobrevivido durante siglos.
Pero los pueblos bien alimentados y sin ideas se pudren en el olvido.
Soy lo que está a punto de amanecer, lo que se eleva en las señales de humo.

We must lure the future and place it between our thighs as a done deal.

An instantaneous life, not a shitty one.

■

Sex is incorruptible.

■

Between gap of thigh and sliver of night, Uxmal.

March 1967

Say of them

O, black vagina
O, red vagina
O, vagina of gold

Legs of ivory
                and nothing more!

                March 1967

■

Thoughts are digested like grain, nutrients equally precious.

People without food but with ideas have survived for centuries.
But well-fed people without ideas waste away in oblivion.
I am what is on the verge of becoming, what rises in smoke signals.

64

■

Llevo a mis espaldas a los que lloran por mis Incahuasi perdidos.

1966

■

Mi lenguaje es sobrio, elegante y delicado como las nubes del alba.
Mi lenguaje es rastrero como la prostituta que intimamente soy.

■

I carry on my back those who weep over my lost Incahuasi.

1966

■

My language is restrained, elegant and delicate, like clouds at dawn.
My language is low-class, like the prostitute I intimately am.

PALABRAR*mas*

**PALABRAR*mas*, 1966–2015

AUTHOR'S NOTE: The PALABRAR*mas* were born from a vision in which individual words opened up to reveal their inner associations, allowing ancient and newborn metaphors to come to light. In 1966 nearly a hundred of these words appeared. I called them divinations and ceased to think much about them. Then in 1974, after the military coup in Chile, they appeared again, arming themselves with a name: PALABRAR*mas* (*palabra*, word; *labrar*, to work; *armas*, arms; *más*, more). A word that means: to work words as one works the land is to work more; to think of what the work does is to arm yourself with the vision of words. And more: words are weapons, perhaps the only acceptable weapons.

E.W.

PALABRAR*mas*, El Imaginero (Buenos Aires, 1984).

~ ~

NOTA DE LA AUTORA: Las PALABRAR*mas* nacieron de una visión: una palabra se abrió en el aire, mostrándome su metáfora interior. En 1966 ví cerca de cien, las llamé "Adivinanzas". Cada palabra contenía una pregunta y una respuesta a la vez. En 1974, después del golpe militar en Chile, volvieron a aparecer, pero esta vez venían armadas de un nombre: PALABRAR*mas*, labrar las palabras como quien labra la tierra es labrar más. Pensar en el trabajo de las palabras es armarse de la visión del palabrar: las palabras son la única arma permitida.

Adivinanzas

La palabra es la adivinanza y adivinar es averiguar lo divino.

¿Cuál es la libélula que se une con el final del imperativo cortád?

Libertad

¿Cuál es la consecuencia de un hombre duro que miente?

Un durmiente

¿Quiénes son los dulces enajenados de color morado?

Los enamorados.

en a mor ados

en amor morado enajenados

Riddles/Divinations

The word is the divination; to divine is to ascertain the divine.

What happens when libido crashes a tea party?
                Liberty

What does the deceitful doorman do at night?
                He lies dormant.

What errs sweetly?
                The Free Reign of Lovers

                in love forever
                lovers ever foreign

Palabrir busca inventar, hallar sin venir, un *etymon*,
sentido verdadero, que ya contiene lo que será.

Ir simultáneamente hacia adentro y hacia atrás.

Considerar el origen
                    es con y sideralmente
                    contemplar el *oriri*:
                    salir de los astros.

Palabrir is to open words

Having lost the memory of the original meaning, we can invent an *etymon* (true meaning), one that contains within what the word will be. To go backward and inward simultaneously. To contemplate the origins and the future. The ancient and current signified.

To consider the origin
           is to con (template) side (really)
           study together the *oriri:*
           the coming out of the stars.

To open words is to open oneself.
Words want to speak; to listen to them is the first task.

E.W.

conrazón

verdad

dadver

aliado

del viento

permite

el dón

corazón/heart: heart with reason

truth: to give sight

breath: the wind's ally

forgive: to allow the gift

E.M.

IN side the VISIBLE

IM pulse of the POSSIBLE

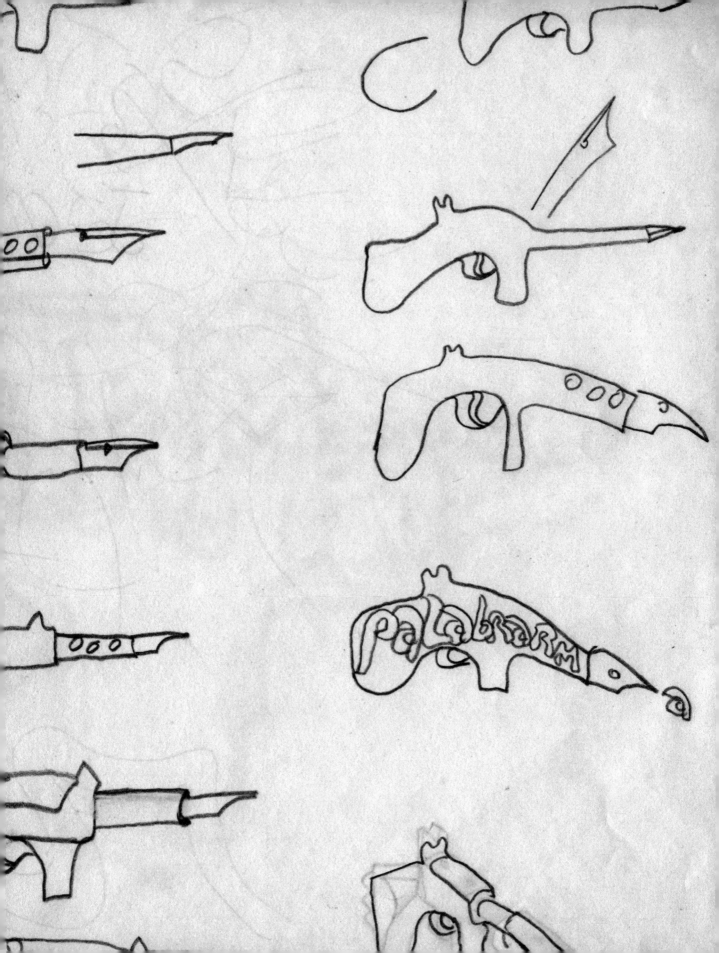

Precarious

Precario, 1966–2015

AUTHOR'S NOTE: *Lo precario* (the precarious) is a way of being in the land, a series of gestures and site-specific performance installations created collaboratively with the elements. Works for the sea or street traffic to erase.

To name a work for its dissolution responds to an ancient vision: the path of the planets, the sun, and the moon are named for their disappearance: *ecliptic.*

The precarious are metaphors in space. They create a history "written" in the memory of the land and the bodies of passersby.

The history of the north excludes that of the south, and the history of the south excludes itself, embracing only the north's reflections.

We are the *basuritas*, throwaways of this world.

Precario/Precarious, trans. Anne Twitty, Tanam Press (New York, 1983).

~ ~

NOTA DE LA AUTORA: Lo precario es un lenguaje ancestral y futuro de gestos y actos que contemplan su propia desaparición.

Nombrar una obra por su disolución responde a una antigua visión. El trayecto del sol, la luna y los planetas, la eclíptica, es nombrada por su desaparición.

Lo precario es una metáfora espacial, una historia escrita en la memoria de la tierra y el cuerpo de los transeúntes.

La historia del norte excluye la del sur, y la historia del sur se autoexcluye, para reflejar solamente la del norte.

Nosotros somos las basuritas, lo descartable de este mundo.

Entrando

Precario es lo que se obtiene por oración, inseguro, apurado, escaso.
Del Latín "precarius", de precis, plegaria.

Pensé que todo esto quizás no era más que una forma de recordar.

Recordar en el sentido de tocar las cuerdas de la emoción.

Re cordar viene de *cor*, corazón.

■

Primero sobrevino el escuchar con los dedos, una memoria de los sentidos:

los huesos repartidos, los palos y plumas eran objetos sagrados que yo debía ordenar.

Seguir su voluntad equivalía a descubir una forma de pensar: los senderos de la mente que recorría escuchando el material conducían a un antiguo silencio esperando ser oído.

Pensar era seguir la música, el sentimiento de los elementos.

Así empezó la comunión con el cielo y el mar, la necesidad de responder a sus deseos con una obra que fuera oración, gozo de los elementos.

Entering

Precarious is what is obtained by prayer. Uncertain, exposed to hazards, insecure. From the Latin "precarius," from "précis," prayer.

I thought that perhaps all this was only a way of remembering.

To record in the sense of touching the strings of emotion:

To record comes from *cor*, the core of the heart.

■

Listening with the fingers, a sensory memory came first;

the scattered bones, the sticks and feathers were sacred objects I had to put in order.

To follow their will was to rediscover a way of thinking; listening to the elements I traveled down pathways of the mind that led me to an ancient silence waiting to be heard.

To think was to follow the music, the feeling of the elements.

This is the way a communion with the sky and the sea began, the necessity to respond to their desires with a work that would be prayer, a joy to the elements.

El gozo es la oración,

lo recordado en la ofrenda es una
forma poética esencial: si al principio de los tiempos la
poesía fue un acto de comunión, una forma de entrar co-
lectivamente a una visión, ahora es un espacio al que en-
tramos, una metáfora espacial.

■

Era natural que la poesía alcanzara una correspondencia
espacial:

si el poema es temporal, templo oral, temploral,
el palacio o la forma es templo espacial.

Ambos templos son entrada al espacio sagrado del
metaforizar;

metapherein: llevar más allá.

La metáfora lleva a otro espacio de contemplación:
con templar nos templa juntos
o templa simultáneamente lo interior y exterior.

Forma activa de contemplación, la metáfora espacial une
dos formas de oración; espacial y temporal.

■

Lo precario es lo que se obtiene por oración.

"El quipu que no recuerda nada", una cuerda vacía, fue mi
primera obra precaria.

Joy itself is the prayer.

In the act of offering I recalled an essential poetic form:

If at the beginning of time poetry was an act of communion, a form of entering into a shared vision, now it is a space that can be entered, a spatial metaphor.

■

It was natural for poetry to complete itself in space:

If the poem is temporal, an oral temple,
the palace or form is a spatial temple.

Both temples are entryways to the sacred space of metaphor.

metapherein: to carry beyond.

Metaphor takes us to other spaces of contemplation;

to contemplate temples us together, or temples simultaneously the interior and the exterior.

An active form of contemplation, the spatial metaphor brings together two forms of prayer: temporal and spatial.

■

Precarious is what is obtained by prayer.

"The quipu which records nothing," an empty string was my first precarious object.

Oraba haciendo un quipu, ofrendaba el deseo de recordar.

■

La ofrenda es el deseo, el cuerpo es metáfora nada más.

■

En el antiguo Perú el adivino trazaba líneas de polvo
en la tierra, como una forma de adivinar, o dejar que
lo divino hable en él.
   "... invocaban a los espíritus por medio de una
encantación y trazando líneas en el suelo".

■

Lempad de Bali dice: "Todo arte es pasajero, incluso
la piedra se carcome". "Dios aprovecha la esencia de
las ofrendas y el hombre sus restos materiales".

Una forma de escritural temporal y espacial aspira a
durar en la intensidad de la emoción.
Recuperar la memoria es recuperar la unidad:

> Ser uno con el cielo y el mar
> Sentir la tierra como la propia piel
> Es la única forma de relación
> Que a Ella le puede gustar.

NUEVA YORK, 1983

I was praying making a quipu, offering up the desire of memory.

    ■

Desire is the offering, the body is only a metaphor.

    ■

In ancient Peru diviners traced lines of dust in the earth, as a way of divining, or letting the divine speak through them;

> "... they invoked the spirits through an incantation and tracing lines on the ground."

    ■

Lempad of Bali says: "All art is transient, even stone is worn away. God makes use of the essence of the offerings and the people of the material remains."

To recover memory is to recover unity:

> To be one with the sky and the sea
> To feel the Earth as your own skin
> is the only way to pleasure Her.

NEW YORK, 1983

A.T.

10 Metaphors in Space

1. Espiral y Mar / Spiral and Sea

En la unión de dos aguas, el río Aconcagua y el océano Pacífico la mar completa la obra, borrándola. / At the junction of two waters, the Aconcagua River and the Pacific Ocean, the sea completes the work, erasing it.

CON CÓN, CHILE, 1966–2006

2. Otoño / Autumn

En junio de 1971 llené de hojas de árboles la Sala Forestal del Museo Nacional de Bellas Artes, dedicando la obra a la construcción del socialismo en Chile. / In June 1971 I filled the Sala Forestal of the National Museum of Fine Arts with autumn leaves, dedicating the work to the construction of socialism in Chile.

SANTIAGO, CHILE, 1971

3. Antivero / Antivero

Antes de ser contaminado el río desea ser escuchado. / Before being contaminated the river would like to be heard.

COLCHAGUA, CHILE, 1981

4. Guante / Glove

En un momento cualquiera del viaje en bus levantaba la mano enguantada en un guante enguan-
tador. El guante no es un guante, sino un ser mítico primordial. (La micro, también va en el tiempo
mítico primordial.)

En el sur de Chile, cuando nace una niña, su madre le pone una araña en la mano, para que le
enseñe a tejer.

El hilo es la memoria del viaje deshilachándose.

During a bus ride I would raise a hand gloved in a glove begloved. The glove is not a glove, but a
primordial mythic being. (The bus, too, moves in primordial mythic time.)

When a girl is born, her mother puts a spider in her hand, to teach her how to weave.

Thread is the memory of the journey unravelling.

CHILE, 1966–1994; NEW YORK, 2011

E.A.

5. Vaso de Leche / Glass of Milk

Durante el "crimen lechero" algunos distribuidores agregaban pintura a la leche para lucrar más. 1920 niños habían muerto por tomar leche contaminada. Anuncié el derramamiento de un vaso de leche y escribí el poema en el pavimento.

> La vaca
> es el continente
> cuya leche
> (sangre)
>
> está siendo
> derramada
>
> ¿Qué estamos
> haciendo con
> la vida?

During the "milk crime," distributors added paint to the milk to increase their earnings. 1,920 children died from drinking the contaminated milk. I announced the spilling of milk and wrote the poem on the pavement.

> The cow
> is the continent
> whose milk
> (blood)
>
> is being
> spilled
>
> What are we doing
> to our lives?

BOGOTÁ, 1979

E.A.

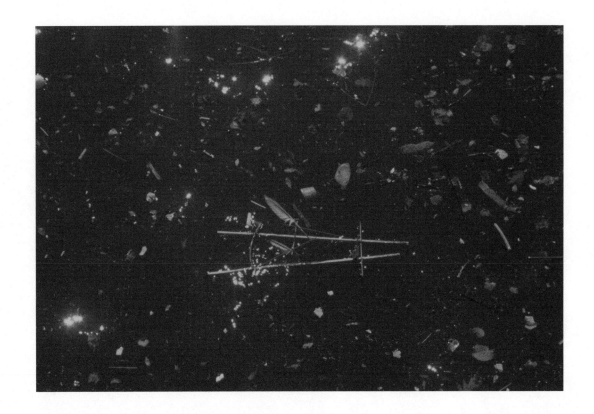

6. Galaxia de Basura / Galaxy of Litter

Signos cambiantes en el agua, mis botecitos y la basura mezclándose. / Changing signs, mine and those there by chance. The boats and the trash, mingling.

HUDSON RIVER, NEW YORK, 1989

E.A.

7. Shadow of a Loom

I set a loom in the street
Looming above
A puddle of rain.

"We are the thread"

                      says she

"To weave is to speak"

Thread in the air
Cloud in the mud

NEW YORK, 1993

8. Quipu Menstrual / Menstrual Quipu

El día de la elección de Michelle Bachelet, subí a la cordillera a hacer una ofrenda, un quipu menstrual rogando que Bachelet no autorizara la destrucción de los glaciares por las mineras extranjeras del proyecto Pascua Lama en Huasco, Chile.

Subí a la sombra de un cóndor tejiendo un hilo solar.

"Re

    cuerda

        (me dijo)

La unión de la sangre y el agua"

"La sed del glaciar".

On election day I climbed El Plomo glacier mountain to place a menstrual quipu, pleading for Michelle Bachelet to stop the Pascua-Lama Project and foreign mining interests from destroying the glaciers in Huasco, Chile.

I climbed the condor's shadow spinning a solar thread.

"Re

    member

        (it said)

The union of water
and blood."

"The glacier's thirst."

NEVADO DEL PLOMO, CHILE / 15 DE ENERO 2006

J.O.H.

9. Río Mapocho / Mapocho River

Nací al borde del Mapocho, un río aluvial que hoy se está secando. / I was born by the Mapocho River, now drying up.

10. Semiya / Seed Quipu

En 1971 propuse a Salvador Allende celebrar un día de la semilla: recoger y plantar semillas.
Convertir terrazas y techos en jardines, ciudades y campos en un vergel! Allende se rió y dijo
pensativo: "quizás para el año dos mil." En 2015 fui invitada a recrear mi proyecto Semiya en la
muestra DUMP! en Aarhus, Dinamarca, dedicado a la liberación de las semillas de los transgénicos. /
In 1971 I proposed a day of the seed to Salvador Allende, to gather seeds and make seedbeds that
would turn rooftops and terraces into gardens, cities and fields into orchards. Allende laughed
and said pensively: "Maybe by the year two thousand." In 2015 I was invited to re-create my seed
project at "DUMP! Multispecies Making and Unmaking," dedicated to the liberation of seeds
from transgenics.

KUNSTHAL AARHUS, DENMARK, 2015

NOTA DE LA AUTORA: En 1980, llegué a Nueva York, pero viajé a menudo al Ande. Mi diálogo con el universo poético Inka dió lugar a "La Wik'uña", un libro dedicado a la complejidad de lo andino, a su mundo de reflejos, donde la luz y las superficies dialogan entre sí. Hay un lugar en Perú, la *Inkamisana* de *Ollantaytambo*, donde una gran roca tallada y vertical refleja la luz del amanecer y el lunecer. Esta roca enorme, vista desde el otro lado del abismo, prefigura el *skyline* de Nueva York, aunque sus escalones no son para subirlos, son *para la luz*. La piedra "germina" en protuberancias que brotan, respondiendo como una semilla al sol. El mundo inka ama la luz y sus reflejos, porque de ellos depende la vida y la germinación de las semillas, y el reflejo principal es el agua, sin la que nada brotaría. El templo tiene unos canalitos transversales que hacen zig zag brillando siempre y sonsonando, porque su canto y su reflejo son la oración que le habla a la luz. Esas aguas desembocan en el *Willkamayu*, el río sagrado, la Vía Láctea en la tierra, eje cósmico del mundo inka.

La luz es el primer animal visible de lo invisible —José Lezama Lima

The Vicuña

La Wik'uña, Chile, 1990

AUTHOR'S NOTE: I moved to New York in 1980, but I traveled frequently to the Andes. My dialogue with the poetic universe of the Inca gave birth to *La Wik'uña*, a book dedicated to Andean complexity, to its world of reflections, where light and surfaces converse. There is a place in Peru, the Inkamisana of Ollantaytambo, where a large vertical rock reflects moonlight and the first light of day. Seen from the other side of a chasm, this rock temple embedded in the mountain prefigures the New York skyline, "germinating" in protuberances that "sprout" like budding seeds hit by light. Its steps are not meant for climbing; they are meant *for light*. The Inca world loves the dialogue of light and its reflections, the germination of seeds. And the principal reflection is water, without which nothing would sprout. The vertical Inkamisana temple has narrow, transversal channels that zigzag across it; shining and singing, they pray to the light. These waters flow into the Willkamayu, the "sacred river," cosmic axis of the Inca world, the Milky Way on Earth.

La Wik'uña, Francisco Zegers, Editor (Chile, 1990).

Unravelling Words & the Weaving of Water, translated by Eliot Weinberger and Suzanne Jill Levine, Graywolf Press (St. Paul, MN, 1992): The book includes selections from *Precario*, PALABRAR*mas*, and *La Wik'uña*, along with new work.

Light is the first visible animal of the invisible —José Lezama Lima **E.W.**

Iridesce

¿Adónde van
los suaves innúmeros

Apiñándose en haz?

La luz
los desea

Y los sale
a buscar

Pétalo
y pluma

Concha
y piedrá

Piel de semilla
petróleo en el mar

Brusco lo brusco

Huequito ancestral

Supina membrana

Iridesce

Where do they go
all those soft rays

gathering in a knot?

Light desires
& seeks them

Petal
& feather

Shell
& stone

The seed's skin
shines oily in the sea

Brusque
brisk

Ancestral little hollow

Supine membrane

Cilia
natal

Rayos radiando

Lúcido entrar

El mismo brillo
sabe pensar

Todo es
sombrita

Cambiante
irisar

Nupcian
quebrando

Su lomo
lustral

Relumbra
huachito!

Ojo pulsar

Entrevera
tu alianza

Poro prismal

Ofrenda
es el iris

Native
cilia

Rays flashing

Blinding entrance

The same radiance
thinks

Tiny shadow
they are

Turning iridescence

A lustrous
back flips

Shine again
little waif!

You,
throbbing eye

glimpse
an ally

Prismal pore

Offering
the iris

Arco visual

Oscura
la fuente

Negro
el brillar

Visual bow

Dark is
the fountain

Shining
black!

S.J.L.

Guainambí Tominejo, El Ultimo Colibrí

Guainambí
tominejo

El último
colibrí

Alentando
su cuero

Antes
de dormir

Chinchorros
perpetuos

Alisos
de lleno

Con tanto
silencio

Y tantísimo
aliento

Guainambí Tominejo,
The Last Hummingbird

Guainambí
Tominejo

The last
hummingbird

Bracing
his skin

Before going
to sleep

Perpetual
swarms

Sleek
full of
wind

So
silent

Breathing so

¡Vengan mis chirridos!

De frente
y de rayo

Bruscando
perfil

¡Aquí todo es bacano!
¡Aquí todo es obeso!

Sombrita
de fieltro

Matando
pulmón

¡Esmoga tu llama
mi picaflor!

Desecho
rubiando

En el basural

Bailando
un reflejo

¡Todos
se irán!

Come squeak and streak

Straight
beaming rays

Sudden turn

Here all is sweet!
Here all are obese!

Dusky
felt shadow

Panting
to death

Smogged in flames
my hummingbird!

Broken
Blonding

In the
wasteland

a reflection
dancing

All
will go away!

S.J.L.

El poema es el animal

El poema
es el animal

Hundiendo
la boca

En el manantial

The poem is
the animal

The poem is the animal

Sinking its mouth
in the stream

E.W.

Las oraciones son los hilos y el tejido es la aparición de la luz. —José Lezama Lima

Prayers are threads and weaving is the birth of light. —José Lezama Lima

E.W.

Oro es tu hilar

Oro
es tu
hilar

Templo
del siempre
enhebrar

Armando casa
del mismo
treznal

Teja mijita
no más

Truenos y rayos
bordando al pasar

Tuerce
que tuerce

El dorado
enderezo

El fresco
ofrendar

Gold Is Your Spinning

Gold
is your thread
of prayer

Temple
of forever
threading eyelet

Your house built
from the same
braid

Weave on

Thunder & lightning
embroidered as you go

Twisting
and twisting

Till the gold
rises

A fresh
offering

Ñustas calmadas
de inquieto pensar

Marcas señales

Pallá y pacá

Hilos y cuerdas

Los negros
y los dorá

Cavilan
el punto

No se vaya
a escapar

Hilo y vano

Lleno y vacío

El mundo
es hilván

Pierdo
el hilo

Y te hilacho
briznar

Código y cuenta
cómputo comunal

The unquiet thoughts
of the quiet weaving girl

Marks & signs

Here & there

The threads & strings

Black
& gold

Thinking
before each stitch

Not to let it drop

A grid
of empty space

A fabric of holes

The world
is a loose stitch

I've lost
the thread

but I rag on

It's a code
and a count

Todo amarran

Hilando
en pos

Cuerdas y arroyos

Río es telar

Aunar lo tejido

¿No es algo inicial?

an account
of the people

Tying it all

Threading
towards it all

Streams & strings

The stars
the river weaves

The woven
woven into one

S.J.L./E.W.

La lengua sagrada, el quechua, se concibe
como un hilo.

"Quechua posiblemente deriva de *q'eswa*:
soga de paja torcida". —Jorge Lira

"Los misterios se revelan al juntarlo todo".
—Robert Randall

Watuq, el chamán es "el que amarra", de
watuy, amarrar.

Watunasimi, el lenguaje principal usa palabras
arcaicas de muchos significados, palíndromes
y préstamos de otros idiomas.

Chantaysimi, el hablar hermoso, es hablar
bordando.

Pero no escribían, tejían.

". . . 'escribían' los eventos sagrados en un sistema jeroglífico compuesto de signos ordenados y
combinados que encontraban en el tejido su más rica expresión".
—Ubbelohde-Doering

Hilo de agua, hilo de vida, las wik'uñas nacen en los manantiales.
Fibra de orar, tejer es orar.
Oro Iánico, riqueza y fecundidad.

"La tierra recibe amor cuando se le ofrece su alimento y su bebida envuelta en paños de wik'uña,
porque la wik'uña es el animal de la tierra".

—Bernabé Condori & Rosalind Gow

Quechua, the sacred language, is conceived as a thread.

"Quechua possibly derives from *q'eswa*: a rope made of twisted reeds."
   —Jorge Lira

"Mysteries are revealed by putting it all together."
   —Robert Randall

Watuq, the shaman, is "he who ties," from *watuy*, to tie.
Watunasimi, the woven language, creates the world
through oracles, parables and prophecies.
Hatunsimi, the principal language, uses archaic words
with many meanings, palindromes, and borrowings
from other languages.
Chantaysimi, beautiful speech, is embroidered speech.

But they did not write, they wove.

"… there was a sacred writing, a type of hieroglyphic system composed of symbols ordered or
combined together, which finds its richest expression in weaving."
   —Ubbelohde-Doering

Thread of water, thread of life, people say the wik'uñas
are born where the springs are born.
Fiber of prayer, to weave is to pray. Spun gold, riches and fertility.

"The earth receives love when it is offered food and drink wrapped in cloth made from wik'uña,
for the wik'uña is the animal of the earth."
   —Bernabé Condori & Rosalind Gow

E.W.

La secuencia del agua

Una
es el agua
y su misma
sed

The water sequence

Water
and its thirst
are one

E.W.

UNUY QUITA

Undísono magma
curvó manantial

Pacha pacarina
esfera y turbión

Una sola eres

Aguaaá

Meandro
tu kenko

Gozo espiral

¿Quién te ensució?

Chichita
challando

Splasha jugando

Tu bolsa
y mi nado
una sola sed!

UNUY QUITA

Curving soundulating
magmatic stream

Pacha Pacarina
flashflood sphere

You are one

Waterrrr

Zigzag meander

Spiraling joy

Who filled you with filth?

Chicha gone
around the bend

Playing splashing

Your sack
my span

One thirst!

S.J.L.

¡ESTREMEZCA SED!

Azapa fecunda

Parina redonda

Sacra cohera

Mismándose!

Fluye
tu siempre

Anda
en tu sangre

Fluyéndose

Taza
en neblina

Tu mismo
ser.

SHIVER YOU THIRST!

Fertile valley

Round waterbird

Sacred you cohere

Being yourself!

Flow
forever

Travel
through your blood

Flowing
through yourself

Cup
in the mist

You
yourself

S.J.L.

¡NEBLINILLA FIBROSA!

Neblinilla ciempiés

Fragando frugando
su fertilidad

¡Cuiden sus llamas!
¡Cuiden su lisor!

¡Qué hermoso
qué hermoso!

Dijo y despertó

Así lo traía
de vuelta en visor

Así lo subía
brillando en su haz

¡Fueguito sagrado!

¡Ofrendilla de mies!

FOGGY LITTLE FOG

Fibrous little fog!
Foggy centipede

Scenting
fertility dancing

We must take care of her flames!
Take care of her smoothness!

How beautiful!
How bountiful!

She said and awoke

Thus she brought all this
back in view

Thus she raised it
shining in its crisscross

Sacred little fire!

Offering of grain

S.J.L.

SE ACABARÁ

la fuente redonda
la propia silencia
la silbida clave

¡Se acabará!

¿Dónde se irá la neblina?
¿La bruma vivificante?
¿Dónde se irá?

Fresco, fresco

¡El sostén de la tierra!
¡Los racimos de llanto!

¡Los corazones apagados
sin neblinar!

THE ROUND SPRING

Its own silence
the sylvan key
will end

It will all end!

Where will the fog go?
The life-giving mist?
Where will it go?

Cool, fresh,

The earth's sustenance
The tear-filled branches

Our hearts extinguished
when the fog is gone!

S.J.L.

Semen de la selva
Semen de la montaña

Donde nacen las aguas
Donde nace el frescor

Dicen los guaraníes del Paraguay y el Brasil: si se acaba la selva, nos acabaremos nosotros también.

Mist is the semen of the mountains
where the streams are born

Mist is the semen of the forest
where coolness is born

The Guaraní of the rain forest in Paraguay and Brazil say that when the mist and the forest are gone, we will all be gone.

S.J.L.

Sementeras de imágenes al sol

Mujer que brota soy
—María Sabina

Hokyani (quechua): brotar, reventar, lo secreto, abrirse la flor

Simicta hokyachicuni: descubrir lo secreto,
soltarse las palabras sin querer

Yacha: saber
Yachacuni: hacer crecer como sementera

Amtaña (aymara): recordar
Amutatha, amu: botón de la flor

"Andar vacío" es no recordar, no tener "flor adentro".

Seedbed of images in the sun

Hokyani (Quechua): to sprout, to burst, to blossom.

Simicta hokyachicuni: to discover a secret, to inadvertently reveal: "to spill the beans."

Yacha: to know.
Yachacuni: to grow, as in a seedbed.

Amtaña (Aymara): to remember
Amutatha, amu: the bud of a flower.

"To walk empty" is not to remember,
to have no "flower inside."

E.W.

Word & Thread

Palabra e Hilo, Edinburgh, 1996

AUTHOR'S NOTE: Its center pierced with two holes and threaded, the book mirrored my installation at Inverleith House, where the walls were traversed with a single thread that began in the garden and exited through the back of the building, like a thought that enters and leaves the mind, then wanders into the void.

Word & Thread was published as an artist's book during the exhibition *Cecilia Vicuña—Precario: Words & Thread* (Inverleith House, Royal Botanic Garden, Edinburgh, Scotland, October 26, 1996–January 5, 1997).

Palabra e Hilo/Word & Thread, trans. Rosa Alcalá, Morning Star Publications (Edinburgh, Scotland, 1997).

~ ~

NOTA DE LA AUTORA: El libro *Palabra e Hilo* era atravesado por un hilo, reflejando mi instalación donde las paredes del edificio de Inverleith House eran atravesadas por un hilo que venía del jardín y salía por el otro lado de la casa, como un pensamiento que entra y sale de la cabeza, perdiéndose en el vacío.

Palabra e Hilo

La palabra es un hilo y el hilo es lenguaje.

Cuerpo no lineal.

Una línea asociándose a otras líneas.

Una palabra al ser escrita juega a ser lineal,
pero palabra e hilo existen en otro plano dimensional.

Formas vibratorias en el espacio y el tiempo.

Actos de unión y separación.

La palabra es silencio y sonido.
El hilo, lleno y vacío.

.

La tejedora ve su fibra como la poeta su palabra.
El hilo siente la mano, como la palabra la lengua.

Estructuras de sentido en el doble sentido
de sentir y significar,
la palabra y el hilo sienten nuestro pasar.

Word & Thread

The word is a thread and the thread is language.

Non-linear body.

A line joining other lines.

A word written risks linearity,
but word and thread exist on another dimensional plane.

Vibratory forms in space and in time.

Acts of union and separation.

Word is silence and sound.
Thread, fullness and emptiness.

■

The weaver sees her fiber as the poet her word.
Thread feels the hand, as word the tongue.

Sense structures in the double sense
of sensing and signifying,
word and thread perceive our movement.

■

¿La palabra es el hilo conductor, o el hilo conduce al palabrar?

Ambas conducen al centro de la memoria, a una forma de unir y conectar.

Una palabra está preñada de otras palabras y un hilo contiene otros hilos
en su interior.

Metáforas en tensión, la palabra y el hilo llevan al más allá del hilar y el hablar,
a lo que nos une, la fibra inmortal.

■

Hablar es hilar y el hilo teje el mundo.

En el Ande, la lengua misma, *quechua*, es una soga de paja torcida,
dos personas haciendo el amor, varias fibras unidas.

Tejer diseños es *pallay*, levantar las fibras, recogerlas.

Leer en latín es *legere*, recoger.

La tejedora está leyendo y escribiendo a la vez
un texto que la comunidad sabe leer.

Un textil antiguo es un alfabeto de nudos, colores y direcciones que ya no podemos leer.

"Los tejidos no solo 'representan' sino que ellos mismos
son uno de los seres de la cosmogonía andina". —Elayne Zorn

．

Is the word the conducting thread, or does the thread conduct word-making?

Both lead to the center of memory, to a form of uniting and connecting.

A word is pregnant with other words and a thread contains
other threads within it.

Metaphors in tension, word and thread take us beyond
spinning and speaking, to what unites us, the immortal fiber.

．

Speaking is spinning the thread, and the thread weaves the world.

In the Andes, the language itself, *Quechua*, is a cord of twisted straw,
two people making love, various fibers united.

To weave a design is *pallay*, to raise the fibers, pick them up.

To read in Latin is *legere*, to pick up.

The weaver is both weaving and writing a text
the community can read.

An ancient textile is an alphabet of knots, colors and directions we can no longer read.

"Today those textiles not only 'represent,' they themselves are
beings in Andean cosmogony." —Elayne Zorn

Ponchos, llijllas, aksus, winchas, chuspas y *chumpis* son seres que sienten
y cada ser que siente camina envuelto en signos.

"El cuerpo dado enteramente a la función de significar". —René Daumal

El tejido está en el estado de ser un tejido, *awaska*.

Y una misma palabra, *acnanacuna* es vestido, lenguaje e instrumento
para sacrificar (significar, diría yo).

■

El encuentro del dedo y el hilo es el diálogo y la torsión.

La energía del movimiento tiene nombre y dirección: *lluq'i*, a la izquierda, *paña*, a la derecha.

Una dirección es un sentido y la forma de la torsión transmite conocimiento e información.

Los dos últimos movimientos de una fibra deben estar en oposición:

una fibra se compone de dos hilos *lluq'i* y *paña*.

Una palabra es raíz y sufijo: dos sentidos antitéticos en uno.

La palabra y el hilo se comportan como los procesos del cosmos.

El proceso es un lenguaje y un diseño textil es un proceso representándose
a sí mismo.

Un "eje de reflexión", dice Mary Frame: "los atributos serpentinos son imágenes de la estructura textil". Las trenzas se hacen serpientes y el cruce de la luz y la oscuridad, un diamante o una estrella.

Ponchos, *llijllas*, *aksus*, *winchas*, *chuspas* and *chumpis* are beings who feel
and every sentient being walks covered in signs.

"The body given entirely to the function of signifying." —René Daumal

Textile is "in the state of being textile": *awaska*.

And one word, *acnanacuna*, designates the clothing, language
and instruments for sacrifice (for signifying, I would say).

•

The encounter of finger and thread is torque and dialogue.

And the energy of the movement has both designation and direction: *lluq'i*, to the left, *paña*, to the
right.

A direction is sense and sign, and the torsion of fibers transmits knowledge and information.

The last two movements of a fiber should be in opposition:

a fiber is composed of two strands *lluq'i* and *paña*.

A word is both root and suffix: two antithetical meanings in one.

Word and thread act as the processes of the cosmos.

The process is a language and a textile's design is a process re-
presenting itself.

"An axis of reflection," says Mary Frame: "the serpentine attributes are images of the fabric struc-
ture," the twisted strands become serpents and the crossing of dark and light creates a diamond:
a star.

La técnica "sprang" es "una acción recíproca en la que el entreverado de los elementos adyacentes y de los dedos se duplica arriba y abajo del área de trabajo". —Mary Frame

Es decir, los dedos entrando en el textil crean en las fibras una imagen en espejo de su movimiento, una simetría que reitera "el concepto de complementaridad que permea el pensamiento andino". —Mary Frame

■

El hilo está muerto cuando está suelto, pero está animado en el telar:

la tensión le da un corazón.

Soncco es corazón y entraña, estómago y conciencia, memoria, juicio y razón, el corazón de la madera, el tejido central de un tallo.

La palabra y el hilo son el corazón de la comunidad.

El adivino se acuesta en un tejido de wik'uña para soñar.

"Sprang is a weftless technique, a reciprocal action whereby the interworking of adjacent elements with the fingers duplicates itself above and below the working area." —Mary Frame

In other words, fingers engaged in weaving produce in the fibers a mirror image of their movement, a symmetry that reiterates "the concept of complementarity that imbues Andean thought." —Mary Frame

.

The thread dies when it is released, but comes alive in the loom:

     tension gives it a heart.

Soncco is heart and guts, stomach and conscience, memory, judgment and reason, a tree's core, a stem's central fiber.

Word and thread are the heart of the community.

To dream, the diviner sleeps on a textile made of *wik'uña*.

NOTA DE LA AUTORA: En 1998 tres curadoras me pidieron que creara una instalación viajera que cambiara en cada lugar y fuera siempre la misma. Medité y ví la imagen de un tejido de nubes cubriendo la tierra, protegiéndola del calentamiento global. Unos minutos después encontré estas líneas del poema *Savitri* de Sri Aurobindo:

> Nosotros que somos los vehículos de una fuerza inmortal . . .
> mensajeros de lo incomunicable . . .
> algún día cambiaremos el sufrimiento de la tierra. . . . .
> el gozo dormirá en el tejido de nubes de su pelo . . .
> y en su cuerpo una música sin dolor empezará a tejer.

Bajé a la calle y empecé a tejer nubes en la calle al pie de mi ventana en Nueva York. Las nubes son "el modelo del refrescamiento y la moderación" dicen los guaraníes. Salí a caminar y encontré un libro en venta en la vereda: *The Maya Scribe* de Michael D. Coe. Ahí encontré a *Pawahtun,* el dios de la escritura maya y ví que su signo era una talega de red tejida en la cabeza.

Invité a mis amigas a bailar conmigo en un performance no anunciado en el Finger Pier de Lower Manhattan. Tejimos con nuestros cuerpos una red, formando un telar viviente. En el video, el poema escrito frente a las dos torres del World Trade Center decía: "Todos vamos a desaparecer, a menos que nazca un nuevo valor neto (el valor de la red de la vida)". Era el verano de 1999.

Cloud-net

Tejido de Nubes

AUTHOR'S NOTE: In 1998 I was asked to create a traveling installation that would change from place to place, and yet always be the same. I meditated and saw the image of a cloud basket protecting the earth from the heat warming the atmosphere. A few minutes later I found these lines from *Savitri* by Sri Aurobindo:

> We who are vessels of a deathless Force [...]
> messengers of the Incommunicable [...]
> one day shall change the suffering earth [...]
> Delight shall sleep in the cloud-net of her hair [...]
> And in her body a music of griefless things shall weave

I began weaving a cloud in the street outside my window in New York. Clouds are "the model for coolness and moderation," as the Guaraní from the rainforest say. I went for a walk and found the book *The Maya Scribe* by Michael D. Coe for sale on a nearby sidewalk. In that book I learned that *Pawahtun*, the god of scripture, wears a head net.

I felt the cloud-net embracing the earth corresponded to the arm setting up the loom, the gesture giving birth to the particle "ar," the root of "warp," "art," "archi-tecture," "order" & "rite" (*or* and *ri,* variations of *ar*), all names derived from the movement of the arm in a loom. A cloud-loom.

I invited a group of friends to join me in an unannounced performance at the South Finger Pier in Lower Manhattan. We wove a large net with our bodies as a loom. In the video of our dance, the World Trade Center towers are in the background, and the poem set against it says: "We will all go away unless a new net worth is born" (the worth of the entire net of life). It was the summer of 1999.

I wrote some of the *Cloud-net* poems in English or multilingually, and the rest were translated from the Spanish by Rosa Alcalá. They were published in the book-catalog of the installation that traveled to Hallwalls Contemporary Arts Center in Buffalo, New York; Art in General in Brooklyn, New York; and DiverseWorks in Houston, Texas (1999–2000).

h
a
n
g
i
n
g
  by a thread

     the
     web
        says: www
            we will weave

     una puerta llorosa
     y piedras en los pies

     a weeping door

           web up
           web on

       re a   lida des
         a   linea das

            weaving clouds
            against death

              c.v.

ar

down an arm

in a loom

setting the warp

in a loom

the inner arc + texture

of art

the echo of hands

in a loom

order + rite variations on

ar

down an arm

in a loom

c.v.

Er

The Three Moerae

I invited a group of dancers to join me in an unannounced event. Entirely by chance, only three girls came: Rosa, Luisa and Alicia. They were late and the place became dusk, darkness became light as they wove and danced.

I thought of the three *Moerae: Clotho, Lachesis & Atropos*

s
p
i
n
n
i
n
g
life and death

Moerae or Fates
they are called
but fate is not
the force that predetermines events
"fate" is to speak
and you fate yourself
as you speak
a turn of phrase becoming blood
your destiny,
to *hit the mark.*

and they came to a mysterious place, at which
there were two chasms

          the myth says

two heavenly openings
and two earthly openings

by one of each pair souls departed
and by the other they came back

       and there

       in that intermediate space

(the South Finger pier in Lower Manhattan a cool summer night)

       in that betweenness

       they were told:

        you will be the messenger

        of what you see

        dancing and balancing

                a thread in the air

bladers passed by
waving their blades

after seven days they came to a shaft of light
like a column extending through
the whole Heaven and Earth

        a beam of light

like a child dancing in the dust

        and here

translators disagree:

a series of circles surrounded the shaft, eight of them,
the whorl of the spindle and in each of them a siren
hummed a note

       el tono es la cuerda, el hilo de voz

all notes creating a harmony
all notes turning a sound
on which revolutions turn

                            "depend," I thought,

harmos

       being

             "a joining"

                 harmony,

                       an agreement.

and in the extremities of it three girls

                       pushed to the edge

spinning of Necessity

               the present, future and past

     spinner
     allotment
     and neverturnback.

               C.V.

Red cabezal

… whenever Venus rises as the morning star
on a day named Net —Dennis Tedlock

La red
no nacida

es húmedo
hilván

talega
deshecha

tinta
en conchal

pensar

envolvente
y tenaz

caer y vol
ver

nectar
y red

    co
menzar

Head net

… whenever Venus rises as the morning star
on a day named Net —Dennis Tedlock

The unborn
net

is humid
stitch

tattered
sack

ink-filled
conch

thinking's

tenacious
wrap

nectar
& net

fall
return

     com
mence

                    nube
                    y cabezal

la red   la niña
es jugar   tejiendo

                    el futuro
                    pasar

un   maestro
lento caracol   de escribas

                    viejo
                    Pawahtún

rastra   el trazo
su baba   inicial

                    la mano
                    recuerda

el antiguo   escribir
formar   y pintar

                    la sangre
                    quemando

una con   el signo
tinuidad   esfumar

cloud
& command

the net   the girl
at play   weaves

future's
way

sluggish   master
snail   scribe

old
Pawahtun

drags his   his originary
drool   stroke

the hand
recalls

ancient   writing
formations   & painting

blood
burns

a con   sign
tinuity   incinerated

la nube
ascendiendo

otra forma   la calle
de hablar   es la grilla

cabeza
del dios

el viejo   en bici
pasar   a comprar

cloud
ascends

a way
of speaking

the street
a grid

the head
of a god

ancient
passage

bike path
to store

Decipherment

"The masculine ah
in the head of the God C,

                K'u, called "the sacred"

and the syllabic sign *na* / house

                were read *ah k'u*

                "of the sacred house"

     a knot
     in the *na*

said *hu-n (a)*

     the book
     is the knot

     and the scribe
     ah k'u hun

          "of the sacred book"

knot book
sexless

the *ah*
neither he
nor she

scribes
equal
in the knotting

c.v.

Ah ts'ib

El libro
es nudo

y el artista
es *its'at*

Escribir y pintar
un solo acto

Una sola inmolación

Un solo
refrescamiento

Volver
a las fauces

montaña
interior

ts'ib

Se pintaban
a sí mismos
pintando

Ah ts'ib

The book
is knot

and the artist,
its'at

To write & paint:
a single act

One immolation

One cooling

Return
to the gullet

interior
mountain

ts'ib

They painted
themselves
painting

dioses monos
dioses conejos
zorro y maíz

Ellos mismos
pintando un ser

pincel en mano

'atributo del dios'

Flor de cabeza

Nenu farero

La grilla es brotar

'Flor y pincel'

nudo son
nudo llevan
nudo a la chasca
nudo malón

monkey gods
rabbit gods
fox and maize

They painted themselves
painting living things

with paintbrush in hand

an "attribute of god"

Heady flower

Lighthouse lily

Gushing grid

"Flower & Paintbrush"

knot they are
knot they carry
knotty head of hair
knot revolt

Its'at

Se acabó
el olor
de los signos

La concha
entintada

Vuelta
al revés

Muerte
al *its'at*

Inquina
y escisión

El saber
se hizo malo

y su olor

muerte
y per se
cución

Its'at

The scent
of signs
is gone

The ink-stained
shell

Overturned

Death
to the *its'at*

Inquiry
Excision

Knowing
made illicit

and its scent

per se
(exe)
cution

Pizom Q'aqal

they say

Force Entwined
Shrouded Glory

A seamless bundle
an open weave

No beginning
no end

May there be only light
                    they say

only continuity within

con
    tinuity

          with a thread

Bundle of flames
Heat within

c.v.

Illapantac

Al canto
se rompen

las aguas
del llanto

las que
media rán

        cantá

        rito

        roto

     la fer ti lidad

el canto
les abre

grueso portal

quiébralo dentro
que hay que llevar

el canto quebrado
que hay que comer

templo e'saliva
que no ha de volver

Illapantac

To song
the waters

of wailing
break

they will
mediate

pitch, a fertile
rite
a little
broken pitch
er

song
opens

a heavy portal

smash it in

it's time to de
cant, to begin
eating

the fractured
song

spit temple
to never return

Illapa

El brillo
remoto

del primer
poder

no el acto
ni el gesto

si no
su doblez

trans
de la forma

mundo
al envés

ni truenos
ni rayos

ni relam
paguear

si no

trás
tocar

Illapa

The remote
shine

of first
possibility

neither act
nor gesture

its crease
instead

trans
of form

world
inside-out

not thunder

nor rays

nor lightning

touch
in transit

el uno en tres

el ruido
en luz

la luz
en ruidal

three in one

noise
in light

brilliant
roar

Dheu

clouds have roots?

           you said
                  dheu
                      at the base

'to rise in a cloud'
as dust, vapor, smoke

'all notions of breath
defective perception or wits'

                      in Latin *fumus*
                      in Greek *thumus*

'soul & spirit'

the breath
        of the earth

its pain

a strong smell

ahora el único lazo que nos une
es ésa tenue nube

   dice el maori.

            C.V.

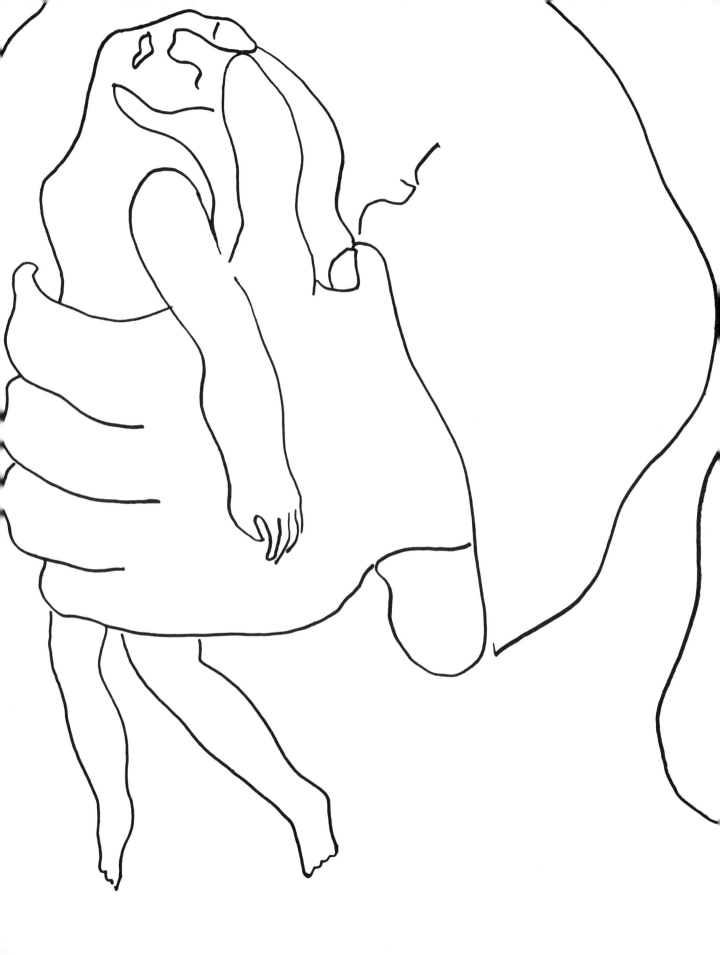

The Temple

El Templo

AUTHOR'S NOTE: Manél Lledós wanted to paint some of my poems. Oh, I thought, paint to poems, as one dances to music! I then recalled Barbara Tedlock's book *Time and the Highland Maya*, which had inspired some of my poems. In the Maya divining ritual, the counting of the days becomes a "speaking of the calendar," where complex mathematical calculations are "danced" by the hands and thoughts of the diviner, who reads the correspondences between the blood-lightning in his or her body and the sheet-lightning on mountain lakes. In a translation across media, the Maya performance reflects as well the thinking of the people in the Southern Andes, where I am from. For Manél, I assembled poems where associations between the body and the cosmos dance.

In 2001 Situations Press (New York) published *El Templo* as a chapbook, bringing together Manél Lledos's paintings and my poems, with translations by Rosa Alcalá.

~~~~~~

NOTA DE LA AUTORA: Manél Lledós quería pintar algunos poemas míos. Pensé, ah, pintar los poemas, como quién baila una canción. Recordé el libro de Barbara Tedlock *Time and the Highland Maya* que inspiró varios poemas míos. En la adivinación ritual del Tiempo, el conteo de los días se convierte en el "habla del calendario", donde las manos y el pensamiento del o la adivinadora danzan los complejos cálculos matemáticos del calendario leyendo las correspondencias entre los relámpagos de la sangre en su cuerpo y los relámpagos en los lagos de montaña. El arte de los mayas traduce lenguajes de un medio al otro en una forma afín al pensamiento del mundo sur andino. Escogí para Manél un grupo de poemas donde bailan las asociaciones entre el cuerpo y el cosmos.

It is close to midday but Day itself is nowhere to be seen. —Dennis Tedlock

K'ij

El templo
es el día

y orar
es diamar,

estar en él
sabiéndolo.

K'ij

Day
is temple

and to pray
is to day,

to be in it
to know it.

Tiempo

El tiempo
es aliento,
respiración.
La noche
y el día.
La cría
en el cascarón,
huevo
en el nido
del corazón.

Time

Time
is breathing,
breath.
Day
and night.
Baby bird
in its shell,
egg
in the heart's
nest.

Ver

La herida
es un ojo,
sangra
la mirada.

To See

The wound
is an eye,
its gaze
bleeds.

Nazca

Torna la mano
el gozo feroz

El giro pensante
de otro rumor

El cuerpo es la tierra

El plano escultor

El clítoris manda

El acto
es la estrella

Fertil izar

Rodando
Espiral

Nazca

Hand spins
fierce pleasure

The murmur
of spinning's thought

The body as earth

As sculptor's plane

The clitoris directs

Act is the star

Fertil ize

Spiral
Rise

Muslo

Muslo rayo
muslo trino
muslo en calmo
y en signos

De raya
y séntido
te marco
       más!

Thigh

Thigh I lightning
Thigh I trill
thigh in calm
and in signs

With sense
and lines
thigh
       I inscribe you
                     more!

Adiano y Azúmbar

Adiano y azúmbar
se huaca el purpur

Temblando siempre
su pobre arenal

Con qué celo
se adumbra

su manantial

Con qué celo
bebe

Su seco
caudal

El manque y el hue
apurpurándose están.

Ancient & Star-Flowered

Ancient and star-flowered
the purpur huacates divine

Transforming dunes

With such fervor
she enshadows

With such fervor
she drinks

Her arid
riches

The manque and the hue
dusking purpur.

Eclipse en Nueva York

Hay entonces esa luz fría,
pensé,
        como en el Cuzco.

Arbol sembrado
de medialunas

Uñas de luz

Sombra prismal

Altísimos pastos
confraternos

y en el orificio
de la mano

Luz eclipsar.

Eclipse in New York

There is then
that light
cold summit
I thought,
             as in Cuzco.

Tree sown
with crescent
moons

Nails of light

Shadow prisms

Tall sisterly grasses
waving

And in the hand's
orifice

Light eclipsed.

Inner Variant

"Bring them to time," Little Nemo said,

      time, from *tem*, to cut.

Bring them to temple,

    a space set aside for con templation.

El templo es el tiempo.
Time is temple.

Dawn and daybreak

timed
  be
    fore
     death
      birth
      a cut thread.

       C.V.

The moon who is our mother, [...]
she made days into living beings

—"Sayatasha's Night Chant"

(translated by Jane Young)

NOTA DE LA AUTORA: En 1992 M. Catherine de Zegher organizó la muestra *"America the Bride of the Sun"* en el Museo Real de Bellas Artes de Amberes, que documentó la recepción del arte de las Américas en los países bajos y la interpretación del arte europeo en América. Catherine incluyó mi obra en la muestra y decidió crear un libro: *The Precarious, The Art and Poetry of Cecilia Vicuña*. Para esta obra hice una "autobiografía en basuritas" contando mi vida en actos que desaparecen, obras precarias en el paisaje, las calles, museos y otros lugares. El relato se convirtió en un segundo libro, impreso cabeza abajo, en la espalda del otro. Lo llamé *QUIPOem*, jugando con los malentendidos y las miradas cruzadas entre el español, el inglés y el quechua. En español suena como "¿Qué poema?", en inglés, el poema desaparece, y en Quechua, el nudo (quipo) adquiere un nuevo final. El quipo, un sistema de registro por nudos fue usado durante 5,000 años en el antiguo Perú, y fue prohibido por los españoles después de la conquista. Para mí, el quipo es la metáfora central de la poética espacial, el cordón umbilical de la imaginación andina, un pensar que conecta con el cosmos y los demás.

QUIPOem/
The Precarious

The Art and Poetry of Cecilia Vicuña, 1997

AUTHOR'S NOTE: In 1992 M. Catherine de Zegher put together the exhibit *America, Bride of the Sun* at the Royal Museum of Fine Arts in Antwerp. The exhibit would document the reception of art from the Americas in the Low Countries and the interpretation of European art in the Americas over 500 years. Catherine included my work in the exhibit and also decided to edit a book: *The Precarious: The Art and Poetry of Cecilia Vicuña*. For the book, I created an "autobiography in debris," the story of my life in disappearing acts, poems, and precarious works performed in nature or city streets, museums, and other places. It became a second book, printed upside down on the back of the first. Both created a composition of opposite, complementary versions. I called my side *QUIPOem*, making up a new word to reflect the cross-meanings of English, Spanish, and Quechua. In Spanish it sounds like "¿Qué poema?" (what poem?); in English the poem disappears; and in Quechua the "quipo," or knot, has an awkward ending. Quipo (quipu or khipu, knot in Quechua) was an ancient recordkeeping system in use for 5,000 years in the Andes, until the European conquerors banned it. For me it represents the central metaphor of the spatial poetics of the land, the umbilical cord connecting us to the cosmos and to the Andean imagination.

QUIPOem/The Precarious: The Art and Poetry of Cecilia Vicuña, ed. M. Catherine de Zegher, trans. Esther Allen. Wesleyan University Press (Middletown, CT, 1997).

Parti Si Pasión

Sex is dust,

el polvo,

the sí

in passion.

And to parti si pate

    is

to partake of

s u f f e r i n g .

(Passion from the Latin *patire,* to suffer)

E.A.

The Origin of Weaving

Origin
from *oriri*: the coming out of the stars

weave
from *weban, wefta*, Old English
weft, cross thread
                    web
                        the coming out
                        of the cross-star
                        the interlacing
                        of warp and weft
to imagine the first cross
intertwining of branches and twigs
to make a nest
to give birth

the first spinning of a thread
to cross spiraling
a vegetable fiber imitating a vine

the first thread coming out of fleece trapped in
vegetation

the first cross of warp and weft
union of high and low, sky and earth,
woman and man

the first knot, beginning of the spiral:
life and death, birth and rebirth

Ceque

there are

still songs to be sung on the other side

of mankind

—Paul Celan, "Thread Suns"

(translated by Michael Hamburger)

The ceque is not a line, it is an instant, a gaze.

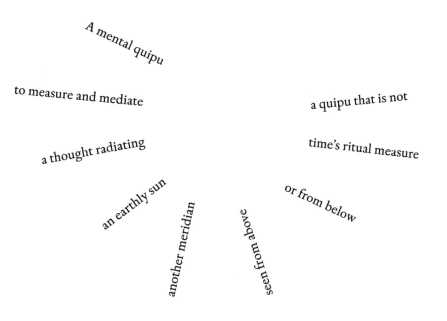

A mental quipu

to measure and mediate

a quipu that is not

a thought radiating

time's ritual measure

an earthly sun

another meridian

seen from above

or from below

E.A.

Cruz del Sur

```
c
   r
      o
         s                    e
            s              h
               s        
                  t

            s
         i           s
                        o
                           u
                              t
                                 h
```

A constellation of darkness
another of light

A gesture to be completed
by light

E.A.

Allqa

Weaving soft ladders   *the degrees of emotion are transformed*

Weaving contrasts   *black & white fall in love*

Weaving senses,   *the shatter is reattached and hate becomes love*

Weaving contraries is the bridge, the bridge of mist

E.A

The Weaving of Words

It is possible to reconstruct a poetic phrase of two members such as . . . 'the weaver of words,' the Indo-European poet himself, wekwom teks.

—Calvert Watkins

teks, to weave, to make wicker or wattle for mud-covered walls, text, textile.

spin, to draw out and twist into thread, from *spen,* pen, Latin *pendere,* to hang, weight, *pensare,* to think.

sutra, thread, from *siv,* to sew, (Sanskrit) sacred Buddhist text.

tantra: loom, from *tan,* to stretch, (Sanskrit) sacred text derived from the Vedas.

ching, in the Tao Te Ching, and the I Ching, sacred book, means: "warp of cloth," and *wei,* its commentaries, means: "weft."

Quechua, the sacred language, derives from *q'eswa,* rope or cord made of straw.

watunasimi, interwoven language (Quechua) is the creative language of the riddles and the oracle.

In the *Popol Vuh,* the sacred book of the Maya Quiche, one of the names of god is "Force Entwined": *Pizom Qaqal.*

Spirit spat out eighty threads of cotton: these distributed between the upper teeth which acted as the teeth of a weaver's reed. In this way he made the uneven threads of a warp. He did the same with the lower teeth to make the even threads. By opening and shutting his jaws, the spirit caused the threads of the warp to make the move-

ments required for weaving . . . he imparted his Word by means of a technical process so that all men could understand. The words that the Spirit uttered . . . were woven in threads . . . they were the cloth, and the cloth was the Word. That is why woven material is soy, *which means "it is spoken word."*

—Ogotemmêli, *Conversations with Ogotemmêli:*

An Introduction to Dogon Religious Ideas by Marcel Griaule

Consciousness Is the Art

This is the spirit never born,
the consciousness of life ...
the bridge that keeps the world apart.
—Brihad Upanishad

Consciousness, to join and to cut, the double movement of the weaver, is the art.

consciousness is	con and scire: to join	and to cut.
continuum is con	tinere, to hold with and	to stretch.
attention is tendere,	thin, tenuis, to stretch	toward

(vertical column between first and second columns:) tone is *tonos*, string, sound, cord, pitch or tone of voice

(vertical column between second and third columns:) string is *strenk*, tight, narrow, strang(le)

NOTA DE LA AUTORA: En mi adolescencia vivía al pie del glaciar del Plomo en Santiago. En verano a veces dormía en el balcón para ver las estrellas y dejar que el glaciar y las estrellas penetraran mi cuerpo. Un día, una palabra entró en mi espacio interior como si fuera un ser. Se abrió y ví el infinito, el espacio negativo entre sonido y sonido. Comprendí que una palabra es el sentido que se teje entre los sonidos. La lengua es lo invisible de lo visible y una palabra es una explosión de conciencia, un evento más allá del espacio/tiempo. Así comenzaron las *Palabrarmas*.

30 años después, la palabra 'instan' aterrizó como una ola en mi cuaderno nocturno, venía del espacio interior, el cosmos del lenguaje estelar. Ví el 'in' empujando el 'stan' y pasé siete años descifrando su significado, para llegar a lo que ya estaba ahí: la estrella interior del estar, *'star'*, una forma antigua y nueva de escribir/dibujar.

En español, 'instan' es la tercera persona del verbo 'instar', urgir, asociado a demandas políticas. En inglés significa 'cubrir de estrellas'. El libro *Instan* deseaba ser un puente verbal entre el inglés y el español, igualmente legible o ilegible desde los dos.

Instan

2002

AUTHOR'S NOTE: As a teenager, I lived at the foot of the glacier of El Plomo in Santiago. On summer nights I often slept on the balcony to let the glacier and the stars penetrate my body. One evening a word entered my inner being, as if it were alive. It unfolded and I saw the infinite negative space between sound and sound. I understood then that a word is meaning woven in the space between. Language is the invisible inside the visible, an explosion of consciousness, an event beyond spacetime. That's how *Palabrarmas* and my awareness of words began.

Thirty years later, the word "instan" landed on my night journal as a wave. It had come from that inner space, the cosmos of language, the word-star. I saw the "in" pushing toward the "stan" and spent the next seven years deciphering its meaning. A new/ancient way of writing/drawing, a *gramma/kellcani* (to scratch and paint) emerged from the quest, landing me at the inner *star* of *estar*, to be, an in *stan*—which had been there from the *start*.

In Spanish, *instan* is the third person plural of the verb *instar*: to urge reply, a word associated with political demands. In English it means "to stud with stars."

Instan wanted to be a verbal bridge between English and Spanish, equally readable, or not, from both.

Instan, Kelsey Street Press (Berkeley, 2002).

compassion

compose

compass

commute

commerce

communi

comb

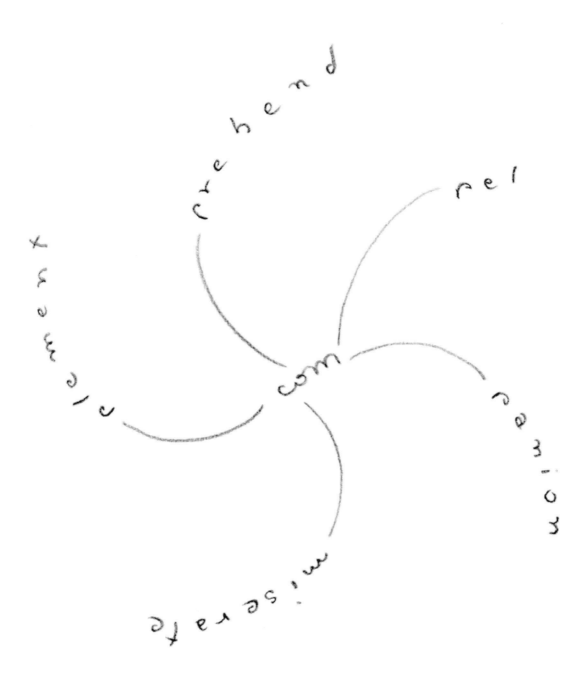

com

rehend

pel

panion

miserate

plement

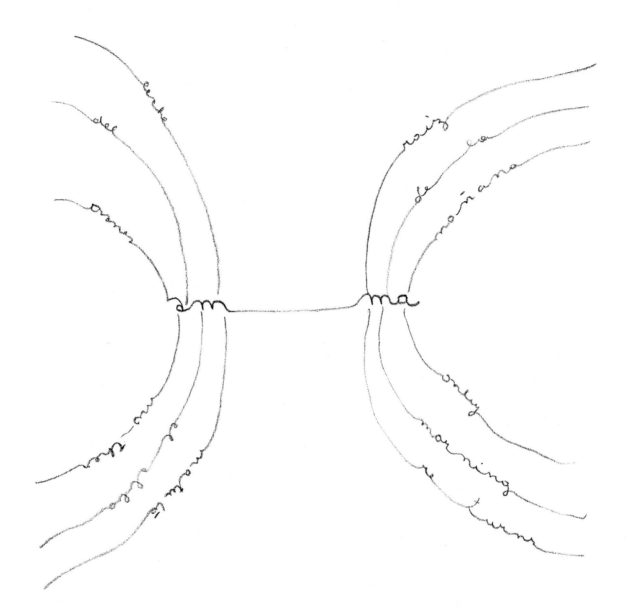

alba saliva

el instan

time bending
tongue

entwine
the betwixt

double
thread

madre
del habla

imán
del gen

palabra
estrella

mother
of time

■

el sign

o

no es

si no

insi

nua t

ción

de la nube

en la nave

ga t

ción

the nuance

of words

the mist

to go through

■

corazón

del aquí

why are

we here?

luz del

portal

mei

del migrar

changed
heart

the in me
grant
      ing
me
life

un creer
en el core

changing
the heart
of the ear
      th

latus del
llevo llevo

mi sed
de un

futur
    o
re late

gramma
ticar

de un
recipro
cate

carry back
el re   late

la justicia
de la relación

la mano
oyendo
un sudor

altas
y bajas
mar

el lápiz
me oye

la línea
oyendo
su manantial

amma

la leche
manando

amar
el formans

gramma
kellcani

draw
write
scratch

el silencio
y el ruidito
del lápiz

son mis
con se
jeros

las venas
del mundo
encantando
su salva t
                ción

escucha
el cimbrar

el instante
es la cuerda
vital

seco fluir
dry elixir

word
loom
star

life's
breath

el instan

estrella
interior

el
  e
    star.

         c.v.
           (Composed multilingually)

fábulas del comienzo y restos del origen

fables of the beginning and remains of the origin

the great Expanse
in a tone Italic
of both worlds
    —Emily Dickinson

O pre-pensamento é o passado imediato do instante.
    —Clarice Lispector

tenderly, between the lines,
                    bled, the lines.
—Barbara Guest

An instant is present,
                    it "stands,"
                                  a filament of sta, a state of being, stamen,
a thread in a warp,
                  a web in ecstasy.

"Being" is a compound of three forms: "to grow," "to set in motion" and "yes, it may be so."

To be not a estar, but a way of being.

Dialogar con lo que no es palabra al interior de las palabras crea la unión.

Opening words I arrived at no word.
A moment of trance where transformation begins:

                                 silence to sound, and back.
An empty space within words where commingling occurs.

Abriendo palabras llegué a una inmensidad.

Our common being: el ser de todos in speech.

Una línea de fuerza que se acrecienta con nuestro pasar. Algo que vive en la lengua y emerge como el llamado de un ser.

To hear its hum, a tongue within tongues.

"Self" is "same," it says,

                        at once separate and not divisible from the whole.

In di vi dual   says

           un divided dual belonging

                  to itself and the whole.

A possibility contained in the name, a pre verbal form becoming "com":
the handiwork of peace, the search for a common ground,

join with,   mutually   comic,   c o l l e c t i v e l y.

En el "con" nacía el relato de una relación.

To carry back is to relate

> a flowing of milk from the tit to the tongue:

> time becoming language and love.

A grammar in amma.

> *"el amor que congrega"*
> dice el guaraní

La leche manando, la lengua y el trans.

Hipnótico manar

> the music of am

El am

> del am

> or

no una idea abstracta

> si no

> una con

> ti nui

> dad.

Migrar y migrar y llegar al interior del estar.

We are only exiled from the inner estar.

> *Love in the genes, if it fails*
> *We will produce no sane man again*
> —George Oppen

C.V.

> (Excerpts, composed multilingually)

Spit Temple

2012

AUTHOR'S NOTE: In 2000 Rosa Alcalá began researching my oral performances and transcribing them from videos and audio recordings, which resulted in *Spit Temple: The Selected Performances of Cecilia Vicuña*, a compendium of her transcriptions and my poetic texts, along with responses by other writers. At one point, Rosa asked me how I became a performer, and I wrote "Performing Memory: An Autobiography" for her. The book includes as well her reflection on the oral performances which I call "Quasars," "quasi-stellar radio sources—the most energetic and distant members of a class of objects called active galactic nuclei" (Wikipedia). The quasar-performances are an ongoing process of transformation, creation, and dissolution, a form of participatory poetry, created with the audience, in the heat of the moment. Or, perhaps they are distant members of Western poetics, or a potential poetic future, or the poetry of ancient oral cultures as I imagine them.

Spit Temple: The Selected Performances of Cecilia Vicuña, edited and translated by Rosa Alcalá, Ugly Duckling Presse (New York, 2012).

~ ~

NOTA DE LA AUTORA: En el 2000, Rosa Alcalá comenzó a investigar y transcribir mis performances orales, cuyo único registro eran algunos videos y grabaciones. Su investigación dió lugar a *Spit Temple: The Selected Performances of Cecilia Vicuña*, un compendio de transcripciones de mis performances orales y textos poéticos. Rosa me preguntó cómo me hice performer, escribí "Performing Memory: An Autobiography" para responderle. El libro también incluye su reflexión sobre los performances orales que llamo "Quasars", los objetos galácticos más distantes, una fuente energética de ondas de radio cuasi estelar. Los performances-quasares son un proceso continuo de creación y disolución, una forma de poesía participatoria creada *con* el público en el calor del momento. Quizás sean los objetos más distantes de la poética occidental, o tal vez una poética futura, o la forma en que imagino la poesía de las antiguas culturas orales.

El Quasar

La luz de un sonido, o el sonido de una luz?

Era su no ser nada aún, su "not yet" lo que me atraía.

Su ser "casi" un borde, un "a punto de suceder".

En ese estado me mantenía, buscando una forma
antes de la forma.

La forma no nacía de una idea.

Era la idea desvaneciéndose.

Al nacer, el "no" la comprendía y aliviaba,
dejándola ser en su deshacer.

Un poema buscando su ser, el quasar no sabe buscar
si no el sueño del soñar.

The Quasar

Light of sound, or sound of light?

Its not-yet-being, its "no ser nada aún" is what attracted me.

Being "almost" a border, an "about to happen."

It kept me there, looking for a form
before the form.

Form was not born from an idea.

It was an idea vanishing.

At its birth, the "no" understood and soothed it,
allowing it to be in its undoing.

A poem looking for its being, the quasar can only search
for the sleep of dreams.

Un poema solo se convierte en poesía cuando su estructura
no está hecha de palabras si no de fuerzas.

La fuerza es la poesía.

Todos saben qué es la poesía, pero quién lo puede decir?

Su naturaleza es ser presentida, pero jamás aprehendida.

A poem only becomes poetry when its structure
is made not of words but forces.

Force is poetry.

Everyone knows what poetry is, but who can say it?

Its nature is to be felt, but never apprehended.

K'isa/alangó

A word moves
a bit of air
   —Nachman of Bratzlav

God is the essence of the written letters
concealed in the dust of the poet's pencil
   —Sumana Santaka

To read a text in Thai is *tibot tack*: to smash it to pieces.

A *Tayil*, a song is "the only material manifestation of the invisible reality," the Mapuche say.

"A song melts the boundaries between the worlds," Lawrence Sullivan says.

A vibratory disorder, an incantation bends time itself.

An image, too, is an "interference pattern," a rhythm born at the meeting point of light and eye.

"We don't see light, we see with the light," someone says.

A word in the air
        lets you
                hear the image
                see the sound.

In the Andes people say an image hears, a textile sees.
(You don't put on a mask to be seen, but to see with different eyes)

But there is no word for "beauty" (a song must never strike a right note)
       you say *K'isa* instead,
       the slow power to transform.
El suave endulzar de una fruta secándose al sol.
Hate and anger becoming peace and love.
A slow-drying fruit.

The spectrum is at work too.

A gradation is an effort of light to unite shadow and light.
"The rainbow has a motor," they say.

To weave gradations is to weave an illusion that hits the eye as a *destello.*

"It is not to mystify with illusion, but to clarify the role of illusion in our perception of reality."

Alangó in Java, beauty, is not a noun, but a god, a divine manifestation.

Simultáneamente arrobado y arrobante, being in ecstasy creates the state.

K'isa, alangó.

      C.V.

NO MANIFIESTO DE LA TRIBU NO

el no-movimiento de charlie parker, ésto somos ñosotros en la noche
desprendida y tibia del sur. mientras la vida magnífica perdure en
nuestras experiencias solitarias y sin embargo unidas, nada nos
preocupa.

no manifestamos ningún deseo o característica. no hacemos un manifies
to para no quedar encasillados. y no tenemos miedo a encasillarnos.
éso es tan difícil como que mañana mismo seamos el grupo paracaidis
ta más osado de la polinesia.
perturbamos el orden con nuestra inmovilidad exacerbada.
además el no-movimiento es un movimiento de charlie parker, de john
coltrane. de nicolás de cusa y martínez de pasqualiz. de rimbaud y
fhiloxenes. más que nada andré breton y hölderlin.
en realidad no nos transformamos en manifestantes para que la experien
cia no sea preponderantemente exterior.
socavamos la sociedad interiormente. por ésto somos subversivos y amoro
sos
además somos tan pequeños y desconocidos que la libertad esnuestro
delirio, no sólo imag nativo. sino real.
las campañas de la tribu no son altamente secretas y los únicos
resultados visibles para los humanos que no viven el no-movimiento
son nuestras obras estúpidas, tontas e incoherentes, aunque no
necesariamente.

damos a conocer la existencia de la tribu no únicamente para que sea
notoria la gran inmovilidad y tambien dedicamos éste aparatito con
palabras a los que hablan demasiado y abusan de la compañía continúa.

esper mos convertir a la Soledad en el nuevo ídolo mundial
                          jo jo
no decimos nada. dejamos todo igual, de modo que nadie pueda jactarse
de haberlo comprendido o agarrado. después de hablar siglos de Ello
permanece igualmente secreto.
el bonito anifiesto sirve para mostrar su intuilidad.
nuestro intento macabro es de ar desnudos a los humanos. sin ideas
preconcebidas ni atamientos convencionales. atamientos=vestiduras .
no se asusten, nuestras obras tardarán años en aparecer: no estamos
jugando. la parte interior de las semillas es suave.
ELLO se conoce únicamente viviéndolo. sea lo que fuere ELLO
ELLO está todavía por descubrirse.

No Manifesto of The No Tribe

charlie parker's no-movement, this is what we are in the temperate and unsettled night of the south. as long as life's magnificence persists in our solitary yet connected experiences, nothing worries us.

we manifest no desire and no characteristic. to avoid being pigeonholed we put forth no manifesto. and we are not worried we'll pigeonhole ourselves. that would be as likely as suddenly becoming polynesia's most daring parachutists.

we upset order with our exacerbated immobility. moreover, the no-movement is the movement of charlie parker, john coltrane, nicholas of cusa, martinez de pasqually, rimbaud, philoxenus, and, above all, andré breton and hölderlin. in reality we are not interested in public manifestations that make our experiences predominantly external.

we undermine society from within. that is why we are subversive and loving. and being so minor and unknown means we can take pleasure in our freedom, both imaginatively and literally.

the no tribe's campaigns are not highly clandestine, and the only results visible to those humans who live-not the no-movement are our stupid works. dumb and incoherent, although not necessarily.

we hope to turn solitude into the world's new idol.

ha   ha

we say no-thing. after speaking centuries of IT, IT remains a secret.

our macabre intent is to leave humans naked, without preconceived notions, without conventional attachments-attire.

have no fear. our works will take years to manifest. we are not playing around. the interior of the seed is soft.

IT is known only by living IT. whatever IT is.

IT is yet to be discovered.

SANTIAGO DE CHILE, 1967

Excerpts from Performance Transcripts

THE POETRY PROJECT AT ST. MARK'S CHURCH, NEW YORK, MAY 6, 1995

SWITCHES TO A SMALL NOTEPAD, AND RIPS EACH
ONE-INCH SHEET FROM THE PAD AS SHE READS

Now I wish to tell you
a sort of not yet poem—
it's about Lola Kiepja
Lola Kiepja
was a Selk'nam* woman
and the Selk'nam
were the first
disappeared
in Chile, that is to say,
they were a whole people
made to disappear

in order to grab hold
of their land, Karukinká

*The Selk'nam people, also known as the Ona, once inhabited Tierra del Fuego (Karukinká for the Selk'nam), an Argentine-Chilean island at the southernmost tip of Patagonia. Anne Chapman, who first visited Tierra del Fuego in 1964, writes that Lola Kiepja was "the only Selk'nam then still living who had been born before the colonization of her land, which began about 1880" (xi); she adds that Kiepja was also the last to live "as an Indian and the only remaining shaman." Kiepja died in 1966. See *Drama and Power in a Hunting Society*, Cambridge UP (Cambridge, 1982).

Karukinká,
which we now call
Tierra del Fuego.
These were not the Spaniards
in the 15th or 16th century
but it was us
contemporary Chileans
and Argentines
killing the Selk'nam
to grab hold
of their land
Karukinká.
The ranchers paid
one pound
per each Selk'nam man
who had been killed
but they paid two pounds
for each
woman
who had been killed.
And the proof of the killing
in their case
was their tits
cut
off.

Their tits.

They were proud of their tits—
to defend their hearts
against
the icy waters
when sea diving

around Karukinká.
Tits with designs
to talk back
to the stars
above
Karukinká.

Then
they were covered
by the missionaries
and no more right
to even speak.
Tits.
No more rights.
Tits.

In her last days

Lola Kiepja

who was the last
Selk'nam
the last person
Selk'nam
the last shaman
Selk'nam
in 1966
she started to record songs
for Anne Chapman*
and she loved la máquina

*Selk'nam (Ona) Chants of Tierra del Fuego, Argentina. Recorded by Anne Chapman from March to June, 1966. Folkways Records: Ethnic Folkways Library (1972).

la máquina
she said
mmmm
la mááquina
that was the tape recorder
she just loved it
and after recording one song
she would say
ORI   SHEN
ORI   SHEN
ORI   SHEN:
that's beautiful
and then she would say
YI PEN
YI PEN
disgusting, disgusting

AS AN INCANTATION:

Atina sentir
tus grandes tetas
mariscadoras
mariscadoras
mariscadoras

ya no
ya no
ya no
su mariscal

ya no
ya no
ya no

naúfragos flotadores

tus tetas

Lola

ya no

ya no

ya no

SWITCHES TO SINGING:

ya no hay mariscal

ya no

ya no

ya no

ya no

con ropa te encerraron

con ropa Lola

con ropa

con ropa te guardaron

te guardaron

te hicieron Lola*

Lola

Lola

mariscadora

*According to Vicuña, *bacer lola*, literally "to make lola," is a Chilean expression which means "to crash" or "to destroy a person."

te hicieron

no

te hicieron

no

te hicieron

no no no

*naúfraga**

aaah, Lola.

*Try to feel / your large tits / sea diving / sea diving / sea diving // no more / no more / no more /sea bounty // no more / no more / no more // your tits / shipwrecked / Lola // no more / no more / no more // no more sea bounty // no more / no more / no more / no more // they imprisoned you with clothes / with clothes, Lola with clothes / with clothes they kept you / they wrecked you Lola // Lola / Lola sea diver // they made you / no / they wrecked you / no / they made you / no no no / shipwrecked.

ART IN GENERAL, NEW YORK, MAY 19, 1999*

With one end of a thread in her hand and the other tied to her ankle, Vicuña hands a segment of it to a group of people in one corner of the room. She then pulls the thread towards the center of the room, creating a v-shaped tether between audience and performer. Beneath her installation—a net of threads that sags from the gallery's ceiling—she arranges a small pillow, where she'll sit for the performance. What follows is a compendium of creaks and inaudibilities.

a   we   core   se
_____messengers of   _____---able
deathless force_____the mysterious steps
_____fog
_____shall change
the suffering earth the light
shall not_____
                        in the cloud-net of her hair
a music of griefless things
griefless things shall weave shall weave shall weave

----------(singing) un poquito un po . quito un poquito

kkkkrrrkkkkrrrkkkrrrkkkkrr   )   you don't hear me?
you hear the floor?

                    (audience: "yes")

*This transcription of the first few minutes of Vicuña's performance (filmed by Francesco Cincotta), which formed part of her *Cloud-net* installation at Art in General, reflects gaps of audibility or intelligibility caused by squeaky floors, people getting off a nearby elevator, and poor acoustics.

la puerta interior de la palabra_____
esta

    art   art

        the arms spinning
setting the warp
_____an echo of the hand

are   in   wri------
echoing

or is a wa------
echoing the arm

----ar-----
the word or_____
only a music of hands

manos_____
crkkkkkcccrrrrrkkkkk
        crkkkkccrrrkkkk iiiiikkkkiiiiikikik ik ik cc rrr kkkk

When I first came to this space, I thought I wanted to do a piece that would be just the
squeaky floors and if I_____you see this is really happening _____noise
this_____
I don't have to do anything
it just happened.

KRANNERT CENTER FOR THE PERFORMING ARTS, UNIVERSITY OF ILLINOIS AT URBANA-CHAMPAIGN, SEPTEMBER 21, 1999*

In virtual reality
somebody said
in a meeting yesterday
as if the World
Wide
Web
the virtual world
of imagination
and the invisible world
of myth could come
to meet

Greed
and deed
the seeding
of seeds
now
HOW
we create

*Performance-lecture, "Seed Speakings: The Potential of Some Ancient Ideas Concerning Seeds," George A. Miller Committee Series.

the ground
for it
to sprout again
the work to create
grounds within
our own grounds
grounding ourselves
we'll give the seeds
a new ground
Thoreau and Emerson said
the study of nature
and the study
of oneself
are the same
are the same
jardinera ven
decinaban decían
germ, germ, germinaban en mí
decían brotando en mí
sprout in me
sprout in me
brotando la imágen
del imán del gen

imán del gen*

the image
is its own gene
its own gene

*Come gardener / they are say-minating, they said / germ, germ, germinating in me / they said sprouting in me / sprout in me / sprout in me / sprouting from the image / from the gene's magnet / from the gene's magnet // gene's magnet

perhaps
a thought
is that seeds
had to go
so far away
from the earth
to begin
to sprout
to have the line
of the poem
go back to the earth
go back to the earth
to fertilize
the earth

WOODLAND PATTERN BOOK CENTER, MILWAUKEE, WISCONSIN, SEPTEMBER 29, 2001

I cannot help but think of the things that happened when we were doing that dance and this is again for the people who saw the film last night. In this dance, we were dancing at the pier, a few yards, not a few yards, I should say, like ten blocks away from the World Trade Center. And so for now for me it's impossible to read this, and not see each time the two shafts of light. You know. This is what happened. You know the towers disappeared and they became this white light going up and I didn't realize of course any of this but poetry has this bad -abit. Or how do you pronounce —Hh-abit. Hmm? Of saying things before they happen. You know? It's a scary thing. And you try not to but in any case it's not up to you, it's up to something else. And so em, I want to read you some poems that were written—here it says '97, so that I hope it must be true. And one of them is a very sad story, and at a few blocks from my place—actually, only a block and a half, this story actually happened. An Ecuadorian me-grant, mi-grant worker was digging a hole for Con Edison, hmmm and apparently he felt very tired, and he took a little nap at the end of the hole, and one of his co-workers came with this huge machine with tons of rubble, and nobody took notice of the little migrant worker sleeping
under and threw all the rubble
on top of him
nobody noticed
that he had been gone
nobody
none of his co-workers
missed him
they closed the hole
put cement on it
night came

and he was missed at home by his brother

And his brother

came to the work place and said:

Where is my brother Luis?

Your brother Luis? Nobody even remembered him

And this is very telling

because this is like our position

the position of the little dark ones

Nobody even notices

whether we are

or we are not

there

And this man, the brother,

insisted: He's here in this hole [TAPPING THE LECTERN]

And they fought him and said no, no he's not

He probably disappeared

He went somewhere else

If he was here we don't remember

Denying the whole thing

Until he pressed, he pressed, he pressed, and finally they opened the hole and there it was:

Luis, crushed, like this

Of course, he was dead

So this poem is in memory of Luis Gómez*

Escoooombro y olvido

sue-ño malherido

el enterrado vivo

*Followed by a reading of the poem "Luis Gómez," a version of which was published in "Authenticating (Dis)Location/
(Dis)Locating Authenticity," *XCP: Cross Cultural Poetics,* no. 8, College of St. Catherine (Minneapolis, 2001), 52–53.

el hombre deshecho
sin cuerpo ni abrigo
viajaaando en el ruido
el hooooombre deshecho
viajaaaando en el ruido

Forgotten rubble
wounded dream you are
discarded alive
man undone
no body
no warmth
noise in transit
discarded man
undone you are

THE POETRY PROJECT AT ST. MARK'S CHURCH, NEW YORK, MAY 15, 2002*

Last night I was a little sick
and they were watching Ali
they were watching, I said
did you notice that? hmmm
They. Who was that?
All my Mes
All my Cecilias
you know
Lying
sick
in
bed watching Ali

Do you remember Ali?
The little dancing feet?
Do you remember him?
I remember we were in Santiago watching him
all of us gathered
hundreds of people
gathered just to watch
one little TV set

*A fragment of this transcript was published in "Global New York," *The Literary Review*, vol. 46.2 (Madison, NJ, 2003), 325–329.

this was the original

TV

set

And was there

We were there

watching   Ali

the little dancing feet

The unboxing boxer

The unhitting hitter

The undoer doing

My GO——D

And when he said

IIIII am pret-ty,

we felt

WE were pretty

When he said I am black

we felt we are black

It was a shock

to come to the U.S.

and realize that we were not black

after all [AUDIENCE LAUGHTER]

hmmm

I wonder who narrowed it down [AUDIENCE LAUGHTER]

We were him certainly

that's for sure

And now I wanted to tell you this story

that's around the Internet

I've no idea whether this is true or not

this is what the Web does:

it undoes the web

doesn't it?

A message came
it says Guaicaipuro Cuatemoc*
had been speaking to the European
Community
on February the 8th,
19
sorry
18
sorry
002.

He said
UsUUUra
brothers
YOU
who ask
us to pay you
our debt
YOU are asking
to pay YOU our debt
in reality
I
loaned
you
millions and millions and million and
ME ME ME ME ME
ME-LEE-YONS
of gooold and silver

*At the time of this performance, Vicuña was unaware that in 1990 Venezuelan writer Luis Britto García had published in a Caracas newspaper a fictional text titled "Guaicaipuro Cuatemoc cobra la deuda a Europa." She read a version circulated on the Internet years later that omitted his name, and like many, she wondered whether it was a true account of a cacique addressing the heads of state of the European Union.

as a friendly gesture of the Americas
towards the development of Europe
this was our "Marshalltzuma plan" [AUDIENCE LAUGHTER]
plan for the reconstruction
of the barbaric Europe
Poor them
But it failed—look [AUDIENCE LAUGHTER]

In its irrational
capitalistic
ways
they are still at it.
Europe always wants more
they need
more
More
more from us
But time has come for Eur Eur
I can't even say it—
Eu You You You Your
Your-UP.
To return
to us
To return to us
the gold and silver
we so
generously
loooooaned
We ask you
to now sign
a letter of inn-tent

as a way to discipline YOU.

Uncollected Poems

AUTHOR'S NOTE: Poems published in magazines, newspapers, and anthologies.

~~~~~~

NOTA DE LA AUTORA: Poemas publicados en revistas, diarios y antologías.

Libro Desierto

Libro desierto
Libro oxidado

textos bailados
y abandonados

libro de nada

polvo y des
pedida

libro de tiempo
y piedra re
movida

libro de aliento

aquí
me voy

escribo con viento
oxidando el tierral

escribo con brisa
entintando la piedra

Desert Book

Desert book
Rusted book

texts danced
and abandoned

book of nothing

dust and leave-
taking

book of time
and shifting
stone

book of breath

here
I go

I write with wind
rusting the dust

I write with breeze
dying the stone

escribo con cuerpo
danzando la marca

escribo con gestos
cruce y temporal

mi cuero
en pellejo

la tierra
marcada

¿quién lee
los signos?

la pampa
tatuada

el rojo
en el muslo

el rastro
borrado

¿quién lee
los signos?

el cielo
nocturno

el polvo
estelar?

I write with body
dancing the mark

I write with gestures
temporal crossroad

my skin
a hide

inscribed
earth

who reads
the signs?

tattooed
pampa

thigh
dyed red

traces
erased

who reads
the signs?

nocturnal sky

stellar dust?

la ella
en desierto

seco polvar?

mano manantial
la ella tatuando

su cuerpo
de estrellas

el clito
la puerta

llave
el germinar

el centro y el borde
gozo
      manantial

hallando
      la hallé
y la vi

marcando
sus signos

la tierra

the she
in the desert

dust-dry?

with fountain hand
she tattoos

her body
with stars

the clit
a door

budding
its key

center and border
pleasure
            spring

looking for her
                    I found her

marking
her signs

the earth

su ser

no la tierra
ni el cuerpo

si no
un marcar

libro
a destiempo

clito brotando

el signo
inicial

her being

not earth
nor body

only
a marking

a mistimed
book

clit sprouting

the initial
sign

Angel de las escrituras, cuneiforme el umbral

Subversion through inscription
Inscription through anticipation
　—Norma Cole

1

Bombardear
el comienzo
es bombardear
el final

el futuro
del humanar

la humedad
del susurro

la sombra
de un signo

fecundando
el tierral

Angel of Writing,

Cuneiform Threshold

Subversion through inscription
Inscription through anticipation
　　—Norma Cole

1

To bomb
the beginning
is to bomb
the end

the future
of human-ing

the dew
of a whisper

the shadow
of a sign

fertilizing
clouds of dust

2

Basalto
de un mundo
anterior

tres piedras
marcadas

un solo rayón

el pensar
de la hembra

Sha'ar Hagolan

cultivos de gozo
y hebrá

cuerpos desnudos
y no guerrear

3

Alabastro
de un gesto
perdido

alabar

Sedimento
del sueño

polvo y polvo
sumar

2

Basalt
of an earlier
world

three stones
marked

with a single stroke

female
invention

Sha'ar Hagolan

pleasure crops
& loose thread

naked bodies
war never waged

3

Alabaster
of a lost
gesture

alabar (to praise)

Sediment
of sleep

dust
plus
dust

4

Corazón de bruma
y estepas de sed

pasan los soldados
los niños piden

                agua
                agua
                agua
tres círculos
de latitud
celestial

              almucantar

5

Angel
de las escrituras

cuña y umbral

"protección y vida"

el signo
en la mano

tres triángulos
aunados:

cuneiforme
"no nukes".

4

Heart of mist
Steppe of thirst

soldiers patrol
children beg

water
water
water

three circles
of celestial
latitude

al mukantarat

5

Angel
of writing

wedge and threshold

"protection and life"

the sign inscribed
on the hand

three linked
triangles:

cuneiform
"no nukes."

Carta a los bosques Pellümawida

Aquí vengo a hablarte *Pellümawida* ahora que se celebra el nacimiento de Neruda

> *Libro,*
> *mínimo bosque.*

Tú *Pellü*, lo sabes bien, él nació de tí! de tu *Mawida*, vientre y follaje, bush del bosque, mata e' pelo. Que si no hubiera andado jugando entre tus ramas, saltando y bailando detrás de un bicho no habría sabido ver ni oír, ni mucho menos oler la vida. Pero dime, ¿quién, en esta tierra, dirá: "Neruda es el poeta de los bosques? el ahora huérfano de bosque?"

En estos cien años casi has desaparecido. Sólo quedan pequeñas "islas", retazos, manchas de bosque donde ver, percibir los ritmos y configuraciones que nutren (*nutram*) su poesía.

Ahora el único bosque que queda es el poema.

Los golpes de luz, la lluvia entrando en el *humus* vibrante, los "relámpagos vestidos de arcoiris" se van.

Ahora sus líneas son la selva perdida, el *mato* del matorral, las frases largas y el ritmo pausado, la lluvia que cae no en la tierra pelada, sino en el *humus* blando, el cuerpo de un reptil que escapa, "el espíritu de un árbol" extinguido.

Bosque muerto.

¿Quién dirá ¿dónde estás? Estos poemas son la guía, el mapa sensorial de lo que fuimos y hoy no está?

Letter to the Pellümawida Forests

Here I come to speak to you *Pellümawida* now that we celebrate the birth of Neruda

> Book,
> minimal forest.

Pellü, you know it well, he was born from you! From your *Mawida*, womb and foliage, bushy forest, bushy hair. Had he not played and danced amongst your branches, leaping behind a bug, he would not have known how to see nor hear, much less to smell, life. But tell me, who, in this land, will say: "Neruda is the poet of the forest? Now orphan of the forest?"

In these hundred years you have nearly disappeared. Only small "islands" remain, remnants, patches of forest in which to see, to perceive the rhythms and configurations that nourish (*nutram*) his poetry.

Now the only forest that remains is the poem.

The bursts of light, the rain entering the vibrant *humus*, the "lightning dressed as rainbow" are leaving.

Now the lines are the lost jungle, the *thick*-ness of the thicket, the long phrases and the slow rhythm, the rain that falls not on the bare earth, but into the soft *humus*, the body of a reptile escaping "the spirit of a tree" which is now extinct.

Dead forest.

Who will say "Where are you?" These poems are the guide, the sensory map of what we were and today is not?

"el perfume del canelo después de la lluvia"?

Tú lo sabes bien. Hace pocos días volé al sur. Casi no se veía selva *Mawida*, sólo bosque industrial. "Casi" es el tamaño del amor a Neruda. No una palabra consumida como un fuego más, artificial o intencional.

¿Viste, ma? Neruda no dice "nativo", sino bosque a secas, o "selva templada". El bosque bosque, bosquífero y boscal, aún no es nombrado "nativo" porque *es*.
(Llámalo "nativo", y desaparecerá.)

Coigüe, lenga y raulí!
Permíteme que los llame a tí.

Amor de bosque, palabra emboscada,
ése sería el verdadero amor a la poesía.

SANTIAGO-NEW YORK, ENERO 2004

"the cinnamon tree's scent after the rain"?

You know it well. A few days ago I flew south. There was almost no *Mawida*, no jungle left, only industrial forest. "Almost" is the size of our love for Neruda. Not a word consumed like one more fire, artificial or intentional.

You see, ma? Neruda doesn't say "native," just forest, or "temperate jungle." The forest forest, forestous and forestal, is not named "native" yet, because it *is*.
(Call it "native," and it will disappear.)

Coigüe, lenga and raulí!
Allow me to call them unto you.

Love of forest, ambushed word,
that would be the true love of poetry.

SANTIAGO-NEW YORK, JANUARY 2004

U.N.

Carta desde las ruinas

Desde allá, quizás sea difícil imaginar la latinoamericanización de Nueva York, las fotos de los desaparecidos en las calles y el terror en el aire. Animitas y altares en cualquier esquina. Mensajes para Paula Morales, Carmen Rivera, Kenny Lira. La ciudad inscrita de mensajes y cartas para los lectores ausentes, los muertos que flotan como una presencia en el aire.

Al otro lado del mundo, en Afganistán, las mujeres perseguidas por el Talibán, arriesgan su vida escribiendo y enseñándole a leer a otras mujeres.

Ambos mensajes se entretejen y elevan como una plegaria común contra la violencia y la tiranía.

¿Cómo comparar el aire envenenado de Santiago con el aire que se respira al pie de la desaparición de los rascacielos?

El olor de los sacrificados lo impregna todo, desde el subway a las mucosas de la boca. Me piden que no hable de los "efectos físicos", pero, hasta qué punto es físico el olor, la huella de un acto?

En la India, el olor es una ausencia transfigurada, un deseo que se anima y proyecta como potencial de otras, futuras realizaciones.

En el Kaushitaki Upanishad el aire se sacrifica al entrar en los pulmones y el sonido se sacrifica haciéndose palabra. Cada acto es un sacrificio y todos nos estamos sacrificando, los unos en favor de los otros. Y esta quizás es la dimensión infinita del cuerpo, la muerte y la disolución.

Aquí, en Nueva York, el mundo cambió, y el que no lo siente, o no lo ve, no lo comprenderá con dos o tres palabras.

Los vedas dicen que la escritura solo sirve para verificar, o re-encontrar lo que uno ya ve. (La ver dad es ver dadera porque se verá). En el slang de Nueva York, el vacío de las torres es el hoyo. El hoyo por donde se deshace el tejido del mundo.

Letter from the Ruins

It may be difficult from where you are to imagine the Latin Americanization of New York, the photos of the disappeared in the streets, the terror in the air. Shrines and altars on every corner. Notes left for Paula Morales, Carmen Rivera, Kenny Lira. The city inscribed with messages and letters to the missing, the dead who float like a presence in the air.

On the other side of the world, in Afghanistan, women persecuted by the Taliban risk their lives by writing and teaching other women to read.

These messages become interwoven and rise as a common prayer against violence and tyranny.

How does Santiago's pollution compare with air inhaled at the foot of the disappeared skyscrapers?

The smell of those who have been sacrificed impregnates everything, from the subway to the mouth's mucus membranes. You ask me not to speak of "physical effects," but to what extent is a smell, the trace of an act, physical?

In India a smell is absence transfigured, a desire that manifests and projects as potential of other, future outcomes.

In the Kaushitaki Upanishad, air sacrifices itself as it enters the lungs, and sound sacrifices itself as word. Every act is a sacrifice and we are all sacrificing ourselves, each for the other. And perhaps this is the body's infinite dimension: death and dissolution.

Here, in New York, the world has changed, and it cannot be described in a few words. It must be seen and felt.

The Vedas say writing serves only to verify or re-encounter what we already see. *La ver dad es ver dadera porque se verá*: Verdad = Ver (infinitive, to see) + dad (imperative, to give). New Yorkers call the void left by the skyscrapers a hole. The hole through which the world's web unravels.

En el umbral del antiguo oráculo decía: "conócete a tí mismo".

Cada gesto, cada instante es el umbral. Y cada uno escoge ver o no.

Pero el que no ve, puede llegar a ver. En ese cambio está la posibilidad.

> *Habito en la Posibilidad—*
> *Una casa más bella que la Prosa—*
> *Más numerosa de ventanas—*
> *Superior—de puertas—*
>
> —Emily Dickinson

C. V.

Los poetas de USA y los autores de las cartas y mensajes a los desaparecidos aquí son una de las pocas voces de disensión, pidiendo la paz y no la guerra.

Quizás del polvillo fino y la persecución a las escrituras saldrá una nueva fusión del acto y la poesía, una nueva po-ética del comportamiento donde la belleza y la justicia del trato sea el único altar.

El domingo antes del 11 de septiembre, estaba escribiendo en mi cuaderno al borde del río Este en Long Island City, viendo el atardecer sobre Manhattan. Mientras escribía la frase: "Dar amor en cada intercambio!", una nube, inflamada de luz, se inclinó sobre la sombra recortada de los rascacielos, adoptó la forma de un ojo rosado, y nos miró largamente. Luego se disolvió y siguió su camino de nube pasajera.

El poema más antiguo de la humanidad, inscrito en una tumba egipcia, decía:

"Permíteme ver tu belleza".

Mahatma Gandhi dijo:

"Responde ojo por ojo
y el mundo quedará ciego"

NUEVA YORK, SEPTEMBER 22, 2001

Inscribed on the threshold of the ancient oracle: "know thyself."

Every gesture, every instant, is a threshold. And we each choose to see or not see.

But if we do not see, we can come to see. In transformation is possibility.

> *I dwell in Possibility –*
> *A fairer House than Prose –*
> *More numerous of Windows –*
> *Superior – for Doors –*
>   —Emily Dickinson

U.S. poets, as well as those who wrote letters and messages to the disappeared, are the few dissenting voices here that plead for peace, not war.

Perhaps from fine dust and the persecution of writing will emerge a new fusion of action and poetry, a new po-ethic of conduct, for which beauty and fairness are the only altar.

The Sunday before 9/11, I was writing in my notebook at the edge of the East River, in Long Island City, watching dusk fall over Manhattan. As I wrote "Give love in every exchange!" a cloud, inflamed with light, settled against the silhouette of skyscrapers. It took the form of a pink eye, and stared at us. Then it dissolved and resumed its path as fleeting cloud.

The oldest poem known to man, inscribed in an Egyptian tomb, says:

> "Let me see your beauty."

Mahatma Gandhi said:

> "An eye for an eye
> leaves the whole world blind."

NEW YORK, SEPTEMBER 22, 2001

Con un Cuadernito en el Met

TALISMÁN

"Escritura para ser usada en el cuerpo"

decía

"the heart of the one who wears it"

pero el cuerpo ya era escritura

de venas y arterias

viajando

en su nunca

acabar.

THULUTH

Neja la forma

nema la trama

Mis líneas

se han vuelto

serpientes

y seres vivos

enrollando

el uno

en el otro

su tempestad.

With a Little Notebook at the Met

TALISMAN

"Writing to be worn on the body"

                                    it read

"the heart of the one who wears it"

but the body has always been a writing

of arteries and veins

in endless

travel.

THULUTH

Neja the warp

nema the weft

My lines

have become

serpents

living beings

each one coiling

into the other's

tempest.

KUFIC

Dice:

"Dios es la trama y urdimbre
cuadrada de una escritura Kufic"

El cuerpo
torciendo

Una sombra
jaspeada

Un veteado
sombrear

Pespunte
y al viés

Ni tono
ni hebra
si   no
su sonar.

LINO

Hebriedad
de la hebra

Linumbre
y umbral

KUFIC

Says:

    "In square Kufic script
    God is warp and weft."

The body
twisting

A speckled
shadow

A grainy
shade

Backstitch
on the bias

Not tone
nor strand
its sound
instead.

LINEN

Threadiness
of thread

Umbilical umbra
& threshold

La línea
nace
del lino

La madre
del hijo.

The line
born
from linen

The mother
from the son.

Des

pedida

(Baile de empellejados y toquío por dentradura)

Habla Gerónima Sequeida:

Des

    pedirse

        es dejar de pedir,

            larguelén la rienda al llanto

            que no es delirio

            eso que dicen desandar:

                  el cuerpo se va

                  y el espíritu se despide

       No es que dios sea malo

       es que la gente está muy moderna.

Leave
Taking

(Dance of the Empellejados and Trance Drumming)

Gerónima Sequeida speaks:

Leave-taking
        is to leave the taking

To depart
        is to no longer take part

            release weeping's rein
            it is not delirium
            what they call
            retracing one's steps

                the body departs
                the spirit takes leave

        God isn't mean,
        people have become too modern.

Oir es el oro

(una respuesta a pascua lama)

El glaciar es el origen de la palabra "cool " y el primer "chill", el hielo lento de una música interior que se muere cuando ya nadie la quiere oir.

Al romperse, el glaciar suelta un quejido, el lamento de una vaca alveolar.

El condor en extinción es el glaciar, el mensajero de las aguas, el intermediario entre los mundos.

Kauri Paqsa, el niño-cóndor, guardián del glaciar fue enterrado vivo en el nacimiento del río Mapocho, en la cumbre del glaciar del Plomo, para que nunca faltara el agua en el valle que hoy llamamos "Santiago".

Fué enterrado y olvidado durante 500 años, para luego ser hallado y arrancado de su sueño por mineros en 1954. Lo hallaron para deshallarlo convirtiéndolo en "trofeo", en "objeto arqueológico". Dijeron: "es el culto de las alturas" y esa frase lo situó en el pasado. Lo llamaron "la momia del Plomo", y ese nombre lo apartó de la vida, pero el niño sigue dormido y su sueño vuelve a la vida cuando alguien oye el agua.

El niño vuelve a la conciencia nacional ahora que los glaciares corren peligro de ser vendidos, contaminados y perdidos. Re-aparece cuando Chile está a punto de escoger entre oir o no oir la música de una antigua conexión con la tierra y el glaciar, el tono específico de un lugar.

Un lugar es un sonido y una forma de oirlo. Un tejido de interrelaciones, una interacción entre la gente y la tierra, el espacio del nombrar.

To Hear Is to Strike Gold

(A RESPONSE TO PASCUA LAMA)

Glacier is the origin of the word "cool" and the first "chill," the slow-moving ice of an inner music that dies when no one wants to hear it.

As it breaks the glacier moans, releasing a cow's alveolar lament.

The nearly extinct condor is the glacier: water messenger, intermediary between two worlds.

Kauri Paqsa, the boy-condor, guardian of the glacier, was buried alive at the source of the Mapocho River, El Plomo's glacier peak, to ensure the valley we now call "Santiago" would never lack water.

Buried and forgotten for 500 years, he was then discovered and torn from his sleep by miners in 1954. They located him only to dislocate him, turning him into a "trophy," an "archaeological object." They called it "mountain worship," and with that phrase situated him in the past. They called him "El Plomo Mummy," and that name separated him from life. But the boy continues to sleep, and when someone listens to the water, his sleep is returned to the present.

The boy returns now to national consciousness, the glaciers at risk of being sold, contaminated, lost. He reappears at this moment when Chile must choose between hearing and not hearing the music of an ancient connection between the earth and the glacier, the specific tone of a place.

Place is sound, and a form of hearing it.

A weave of interrelations, interactions between people and land, the space of naming.

Cambiar el significado de un nombre es cambiar el mundo.

En el Alto del Carmen, en el Valle del Huasco, la tierra de los antepasados de Gabriela Mistral, Chile está escogiendo un sentido. "Alto del Carmen" podría ser el lugar donde Chile pone en alto su poesía, o podría ser el fin de la poesía.

Hoy, los pastores huascoaltinos, descendientes de los diaguitas, son los guardianes de la antigua visión del glaciar como el lugar sagrado que garantiza la vida. Podemos escoger oir la música del lugar, en todo su potencial, o poner fin a la vida entregando el glaciar y las minas al poder neocolonial.

Pero, ¿oímos su voz? o nuestra propia voz interior? u oímos la voz del sistema que dice: "El dólar es lo que vale" "Ustedes, qué saben". "Ahora nosotros somos los dueños de las minas y el cianuro es el nuevo guardián de las aguas".

> El agua es el oro
> Manquemilla
>
> La sangre del glaciar
> Oyéndonos.

Los hielos que se desplazan lentos son el testimonio de una antigua relación con la tierra y el agua, y el mantenimiento ritual de su fluidez, nuestro verdadero patrimonio cultural. La herencia futurista de una música que sustenta la tierra y la vida humana a la vez.

En Australia, los pueblos originarios recuperaron la dignidad y la propiedad de la tierra a través de la poesía: el mantenimiento ritual de sus historias en el paisaje: su "songline".

En Chile, el cóndor y el agua de las historias, la memoria del pueblo es el "songline", la línea de un canto que entra en la tierra fecundándola.

El quipu inasible de nuestra continuidad.

2006

To change the meaning of a name is to change the world.

In Alto del Carmen, situated in the Huasco Province, land of Gabriela Mistral's ancestors, Chile must decide on a meaning. Alto del Carmen could be the place Chile chooses to honor its poetry above all else. Or, it could be the end of poetry.

Today, shepherds from Valle del Huasco, descendants of the Diaguita, are guardians of an ancient vision of the glacier as life-giving, sacred. We can choose to listen to the music of the place, in all its potential, or put an end to life by surrendering the glacier and the mines to neocolonial powers.

But do we hear its voice? Our own interior voice? Or do we hear the voice of a system that says, "The dollar is what counts" "What do you know?" "We are now the owners of these mines, and cyanide is the new guardian of the waters."

> Water is gold
> Manquemilla, Gold Condor
>
> The blood of the glacier
> listening to us.

The slowly shifting ice is testimony to an ancient relationship with earth and water, and ritual conservation of its fluidity is our true cultural patrimony. The future inheritance of a music that sustains the earth and human life simultaneously.

In Australia, indigenous peoples have recovered their dignity and their land rights through poetry: the ritual conservation of their history in the landscape is their "songline."

In Chile, the condor and the water of legends, the memory of the people, is the line of song that enters the earth to fecundate it.

The intangible quipu of our continuity.

2006

Quen-to Shipibo

FOR ROSA ALCALÁ

Y las dos eran ninguna
—Federico García Lorca

I am not making art, I am making myself
—Nam June Paik

Dos líneas
tocando
un cánta
      ro
        en lados opuestos

two women
singing

a thought
        twining
a meeting
      of souls

              el deseo
              es el arte

              quene- quentó
pinta que pinta

el cánta
      ro
healing
      ro nin
           lines are que-ne
           un deseo de amor
           lines are quen-tó

shina tus thoughts
el deseo

shining across
la fibra
      kikin ainbó

Wawantita marca
la vieja entrevera

sus signos quebrados
tocando la unión

la hija sin madre
la madre sin hija

solo ella
is free

to break open
her thoughts

only she
brings forth

invisible crowns
invisible works

la fuerza e' la unión

one design
que-ne maití.

c.v.

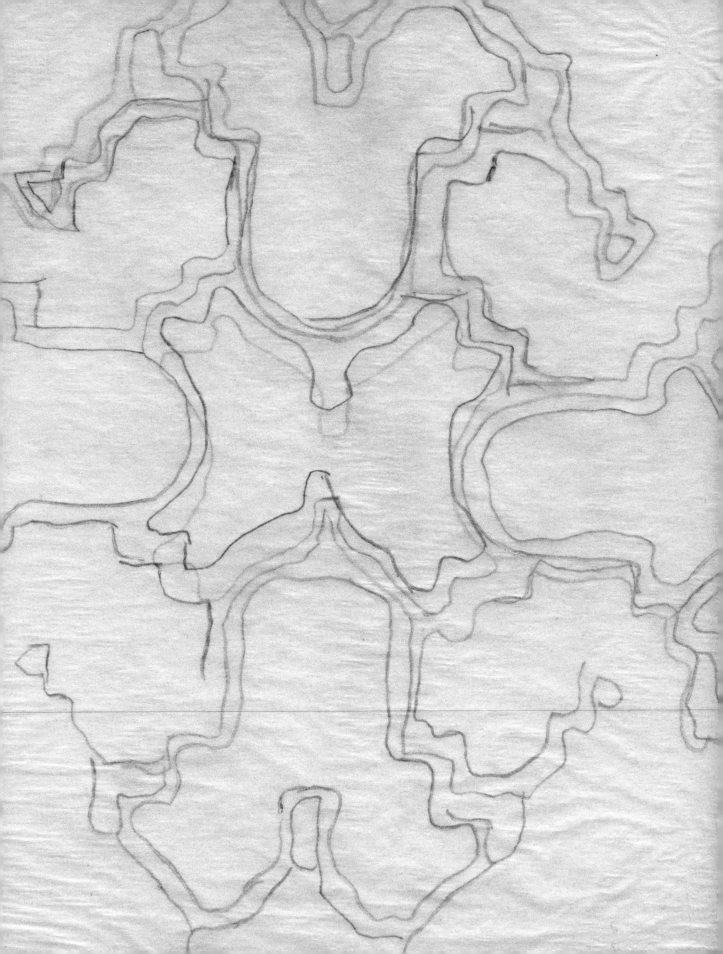

Mete o rito/
Agustina
Quinchamal

quién
piedra

quién
habla

quién
tiempo

trenza
e mete
o rito

chapelen

pillan
toqui

Agustina
Quincha
mal

Mete o rite/
Agustina
Quinchamal

who
stones

who
speaks

who
times

braids
of mete
or rite

chapelen

pillan
toqui

Agustina
Quincha
mal

niña
pareada
lengua
raza

pintora
e quillango

palabra
estrella

sin mete
o rito

la gente
tehuel

che

todo
perdió.

paired
girl
tongue woman
race interpreter

woman painter
of hides

word
star

without mete
or rite

her people
southern

folk

lost
everything.

Esas notas absurdas

1

La mano respira su ritmo innato y el ojo la mira mirar deslizándose sobre el papel.

2

Un puñado de formas, chales abiertos sin principio ni fin, chaquetitas breves con trenzas por encima y bordes entradizos, dados vueltas, a las apuradas y sin terminar. Un agregado suntuoso al arte de la basura, un taller de des-arme en cierne, un capítulo de sangre distendida por el golpe y la pregunta, la secuencia de racimos desgastados, anónimos, fortuitos. Una escalera des-garrándose viento abajo, en sordera, en especie blanda, no oir nada, hacer como si nada, que lloviera y eternamente, más plata des-gajada, saliéndose de borde, quicio y marea, volviendo a empezar.

3

Todo se exalta y agujerea mientras miro y me adelanto en el gozo, rutilo, mutilo de viento mis propios labios alborozados incomiendo indolando su propia labia, juguera instantánea, decían de puro gusto, de puro gozo malsano salucidando su manera: el gozo manual.

Se sobresalta haciendo su bienestar, se dulcinea, embelesa por dentro dejándose estar, embriangando la frente, los labios del ésto mirar.

La boca mira su futuro tragar lo entra nalgando, fragua contenta y chirria en zig-zag.

Es que vi un cuerpo ganoso, desiderándose, empotándose, diestro, inverado en el agua del desposar, el frígido linfando, el que fiesta su voz, sacando su mole, su cresta de . . . su molida peste, esmirria, aporía.

Those Absurd Notes

1

The hand breathes its innate rhythm, and the eye watches it, its gaze gliding across paper.

2

A fistful of forms, shawls unfurled without beginning or end, slender jacket topped with braids, seams turned inside out, exposed, hastily sewn and unfinished. A sumptuous addition to garbage art, a nascent disarmament workshop, a chapter of blood yielded in question and blow, a series of clusters, anonymous, worn, fortuitous. Stairs collapsing downwind, into deafness, into soft forms, to hear nothing, act as if nothing, that it would rain and eternally silver slivers, to cross the line, unhinge, move against the tide. And begin again.

3

Everything intensifies and pierces as I watch and advance in pleasure, moistening and mutilating with wind jubilant lips as they ingestulate their proper flesh, instant juicer they proclaim out of pure delight, pure perverse pleasure, hellocinating in their own manner: manual pleasure.
It startles itself with the wellness of its making, self-sweetens, bewitches from within allowing its stay, it intoxicates the forehead, the lips of this looking.
The mouth watches its future swallow, enters it from behind, forges happily and in zigzag squeals. What I saw was a lively body desiring itself, libido-lit, bedexterous, engulfed in conjugal waters, lymphing behind its frigid, its feted voice, its raised mound and crown ... its funk ground down, its scrawny aporia.

No ví, saliendo su cara, su pues hirsuta, tu nunca estás.

Me cimbro en tu golpe, mi-jito. Alguien se mueve danzando adentro de la casa (cocinando y bailando de gusto).

Alguien adentro de una situación cotidiana se convierte en mariposa.

I did not see, as its face appeared, its hirsute well-then, your never-around.

You pound and I pulsate,
my dear. Someone inside the house shimmies (joyfully cooking and dancing). Someone in a domestic setting turns butterfly.

DISPROSODIAS o San Visiones tras TOCADAS de Xul Solar

Escribo estas líneas en el día de la tormenta más grande de la historia: comienza el futuro con el huracán Sandy azotando Manhattan.

HEXAGRAMA 25 / DEL I CHING: WU WANG / LA INOCENCIA (LO INESPERADO)

El cielo en lo alto, abajo, lo emergente. Cuando la ley cósmica domina, el ser es inocente y su mente se libera de propósitos ulteriores.

1

En una pampa vacía se acaba nuestra vida, progérseme un acento rayo, un fu'i divo semihumano, acercándome, yuxtafloto, en su rédor todo son flamas, el divo está hecho de manrestos revuelvios, suma de lo muerto-vivo, ahí quntios, los restos son re-vivibles por magia y memoria. La lumbre de un recuerdo, la magnitud humana los reanima, veo el gluon, la fuerza que los une, se fluiden, entón, la gente despierta.

2

La fueicidá, la ciudad que fue fuego y ya no es, la ciudad muerta, que ya no será, gloméría plur' dispisoh, suibáus. Casas sui generis no hay nadie, todo se ha ido. El fueidivo pálido, pierde su mampecho, su humanidad se apaga y un lumiglobo se enciende de otredad, su fóspiel fosforescente ilumina lo que será.

DISPROSODIES or Saint Visions, after TOCADAS by Xul Solar

I write these lines on the day of Hurricane Sandy, the biggest storm in history, the beginning of the future, lashing Manhattan.

HEXAGRAM 25 / WU WANG / INNOCENCE (THE UNEXPECTED)

Heaven is above; movement is below. When movement follows the law of heaven, man is innocent and without guile.

1

On an empty pampa a lightning accent protexts me, an alloffire semi-human god approaching me, juxtafloating, round him all are flames, the god is made of admixed manremains, the whole of living-dead, jointup there, the remains to be revived by magic and memory. The glow of a recollection, human magnitude reanimates them, I see the gluon, the strength that unites them, fluidify, & so, people awaken.

2

Firecide, the city that was fire and is no more, the dead city that will no longer be, glomeration plurdisposedof, outswept. Theres no one, everythings gone. The pale alloffiregod loses his mater-breast, his humanity is extinguished and a lumiglobe lights up with otherness, his phoskin phosphoresces lighting up that which will be.

3

Ay fuente de fueiagua futura, fuente del es, adónde estás en el peregrino perder?

En lo que se hunde y se va? Algo me lleva y me sumerge en el fuego, kemipureme, el fuego me limpia y no sentu nada. Para ver meqor i ser otro imagino el no ser, el entretanto del que dejé y del que seré, ahí debu autoflamiar, iluminar-me por mí mismo. Entonces sé, eso es la vida! Lu exo, lo de fuera noh signifi ca nada si no lo coséntamo, lo cosentimos, alfin flameu algo, amar lo divino me enciende, menfoge, no soy sino el pensifuego, lo que arde y brilla en el no ser, el pensifuego que satur'este espasio. Kieru ver la gente deakí, enjambres de fluseres casinformes, más bien. Oh, plen'-sueñin, vivoh soñindo, viendo otra gente que no es gente sino estrella.

4

Perdío en los man-co-astros, la suma de lo humano y lo estelar, oigo el audu del ser: "teós es pandiós" i debe ser teokai aki, adorado, exaltado: oriluznúcleo dice la luz del ahora es el núcleo, el brillar no impedido, la luz de los seres plur'otros, llenos de otros, sumas de otros, los que son luz del otro, lu del hintercruze mas brille, (los que se tocan y se intercruzan brillan más, aún separados como están) ambos copuntos, tamién los veu húnidos num mismo punto, qum punto, por una surdi-mensión, supra escala no calculable, infinito interior fosgrís.

HEXAGRAMA 24 FU/EL PUNTO DE CAMBIO (PROFECÍA DEL OCUPA)

Cuando las líneas oscuras han expulsado a las líneas de luz, otra luz viene de abajo.

1

entru en forma de ciempies vital por la puerta deste signo.

3

Oh fount of future fierywater, fount of it, where are you in your wandering loss? In what sinks and goes away? Something draws me on and sinks me into fire, chemipurifying, the fire cleanses me and I dont feel a thing. The betr to see & be another I imagine nonbeing, the mean-while of who I left and who I'll be, here I shud selfflameup, illuminate-myself on my own. The exo, the outside dusnt mean anything if we don't withfeel it, I with-feel and at last I flaym something, loving the divine lights me up, meupfires, I am only the firethought, what burns and shines in nonbeing, the fire-thought that saturatthis space. I whish to see the people fromere, swarms of quasunformed flowbe-ings, rather. Oh, fullondreemlet, I liv by dreeming, seeing other people who are not people but star.

4

Lost in the one-hand-stars, sum of the human and the stellar, I hear the audible being: "deity is pan-deity" & it must be theokai here, adored, exalted, goldenlightnucleus says the light of now, unim-peded shining, light of the plurother beings, filled with others, totalities of others, those who are the light of the other, those of the hintercrossing shine brighter (those who touch each other and cross each other shine more brightly, though separated), both copoints, I allso si them sunq into the same point, one point, through a superdimension, above an incalculable scale, an infinite inner phosgrey.

HEXAGRAM 24 FU / RETURN (THE TURNING POINT) / (PROPHECY OF OCCUPY)

When the dark lines have pushed all of the light lines upward and out of the hexagram, another light line enters the hexagram from below.

1

i intro in the shape of a vital centipede through the door of this sign.

2

serebro mui pensin   cerebro muy pensador

cuore mui séntuedo   corazón muy sentidor

pierdo la forma

yo kiz, yo quizás también sou un dios

ocupin   infinito   cosmos

ocupar es el cosmos!

hor   luz   túberes

papitas doradas de luz arrobándose en paz

HEXAGRAMA 3 CHUN: DIFICULTAD EN EL COMIENZO /AR QUI TEC TURAS

El brote nuevo choca con un obstáculo. Después de la tormenta el brote

comienza a brotar.

1

oh oh   ojo   los inundados aún no quieren ver!

espumas i olicrestas destellan a destiempo. en la tempestad interior seres solos

emiten luz. ¿en qué está esta solida mundiurbe que no conecta con esta bría, esta fuerza kes aora

lo real?

2

veri thinqing braine	very thinking brain
veri feelful harte	very feeling heart

i lose shape
i whoam a god aswell

occupy   infinite   cosmos

occupying is the cosmos!

hou   light   tubers

peacefully enraptured little potatoes golden with light

HEXAGRAM 3 CHUN / DIFFICULTY AT THE BEGINNING (AR CHI TECT TURES)

A blade of grass pushes against an obstacle as it sprouts out of the earth. A thunderstorm brings release from tension, and all things breathe freely again.

1

eeh aye eeh   eye   the flooded ones still do not want to see!

foams and wavecrests sparkle inopportunely, in the internal storm lone beings emit light. what is in this solid globacity that does not connect to this force, this strength whichz now whatz real?

2

Flotisalgo a gran weco de aire blugris con misma tempestá, vientos más densos.

3

Porfin llega una procesión, seres yunpénsido, pensando como uno, pensadores en círculo, nácar y fieltro!

4

Me axu en cielo leve celeste. las plantas se biomovan i canturrian.

5

Dootri lado hay un templo flotante, muchos rezan, en su teocó tocan el dios,
se sanexaltan, participan de lo divino y sus auras manan prana.

6

Dootri lado una torre de libros, pri petri, epi, tijol, xy'l epi, rolhi, hi.
Letras como moscas perivuelan en letri enxambres a su redor.

7

Arqui tec turas vivas, biopalacios i biochozas armadas quizás de alma y pensamiento percamban en biocúmulos temblequean se mudan, suben, se interpenetran y flotan por sí mismas.

2

Floatsathing with a large hole of blugrey air with same stoorrmm, denser winds.

3

Finally a procession arrives, beings neerthotof, thinking as one, thinkers in a circle, mother-of-pearl and felt!

4

I soor into light celestial sky, plants biomove & hum.

5

Fromtother side is a floating temple, many pray, in their theo-co they touch the god, they saintexult, participate in the divine and their auras flow with prana.

6

Fromtother side a tower of books, pri petri, epi, tijol, xy'l epi, rolhi, hi.
Letters like flies perisoar in letred swarmz allround.

7

Living archi tec tures, biopalaces and biohuts armed perhaps with soul and thought thruchange into biocumuli quiver move about rise up, interpenetrate and float on their own.

8

Casas ai ke ardan, pero no se destruian, se ne 'truyan, se construyen más.

Su fuego es vita i a mayor encendio más palacio. Su gente tamién coflamea.

Casas y gente hierven de fervor, estallan de amor, humoy géisir de amor. No se destruyen, se

re'truyen, diversas y amontonadas crezijuntas fervicrecen sucursales de amor.

9

Casas ai ke sui crezan, crecen por sí mismas, zonti, bies, upa, yuso, gordi: hi zumban chirrian cruxan,

hablan en lenguas dislalan.

10

El suelo desta ciudá es una nube plural.

Bajo esa ciudá hai otra ciudá al revés.

Hosca, lenta, oscura y viva creza para abajo.

11

Reveu la otra ciudá upa. La ciel'chusma, chusma del cielo hautofeliz, revuelta

en bruma y coágulos: bocetos de penso i noia fumifango.

Hai teocahlis aztecas solo de lenguas' libro do sencuerpan sus lectores ke no leen

si nó ke chupan fuerzas, el brío vital, el jugo de lenguas.

12

Sexpandan ondulan vozeríos de tuas las linguas con sus letras enxambres marañas glifos y disproso-

dias. Contrapuntean, co-, dis, re, forman senso y argu

siempre nuevo.

8

Houses here be burning, but not destroyed, constructed more than structed. Their fire is lyfe & the greater the burn the greater the palace. The people co-flame aswell. Houses and people boil with fervor, explode with love, smoke and geyser of love. Various and piledup togethergrown fervisprouting local offices of love.

9

Houses here be growing, growing on their own, zonti, bies, upa, yuso, gordi: here they buzz squeak crow speak in consodissonant tongues.

10

The ground of this citie is a plural cloud.
Under this citie be another upside down citie.
Gloomy, slow, dark, and alive downward growing.

11

I seegain the other citie, the rabble sky, rabble of the happyhigh sky, clouded with fog and coagulates: outlines of thought and smokymud ennui. Here be Aztec teocallis only of book tongues whar their readers embodify, not reading but sucking forces, vital brio, juice of languages.

12

Sexpanding undulating spokers of all linguages with their swarms of letters thickets glyphs and disprosodies. Counterpointing they co-, dis-, re-form sense and ever new lingold.

C.W.

The Melody of Structures

healing is a pervasive force
—Emma Kunz

A desire for completion, healing is wholing.

The eye heals the drawing with its gaze.

To complete the silence that wants to speak.

A divination that she unfolds in the line and its intersection.

The line is the labyrinth, said Borges, and I'm on my way.

Weaving baskets of thoughts, Emma Kunz entered the line
as one enters a garden.

A force field, the line is a multidimensional space.

Transcription and theater of thinking.

The energy of thought is Emma Kunz's medium and material.

Aristotle invented the word energy, *energeia*, pulling it from
en ergon, like thread from fleece.

En ergon: at work

Energía works like all of us, and its *werg* is "to do."

Work & worship stem from the same *werg*.

The *org* of secrets, an orgy of organization,
the orgiastic work of adoration!

Enorgía del bien!

To draw is *tragh*, drag, extract something from one's self
that begins to live when you draw it out.

A drawing works to transform.

> "Angular forms combat negative forces"

> "Soft forms work in healing."
> —Emma Kunz

Her method is her melody.
Search and measure.

A going after, in pursuit.

The "mode" of doing something is its medicine.
Method and mode, from *mederi,* to look after and heal.

> "New intersections must be generated consciously"
> —Emma Kunz

Work that is only accomplished sharing its *ergon*, working with it.

in   tense

woven   baskets

of thought

A drawing waits.

Drawing and reader—forms of energy crossing.

Perhaps that is why she didn't transcribe the words she used to discuss her work, to not limit the reader's freedom.

Hoping each would arrive naked at the line?

Naked and newborn, without preconceptions, like Lezama Lima said:

"to be ancient at night and newborn by day."

Or was she waiting for a new kind of speech? A textile tongue for the inner forces of speech to vibrate?

A metaphor aware of itself. Not a precise form, but a form in search of precision?

A suggestion moves underneath, rising when drawn.

In healing, she placed the drawing on the floor, next to the patient, and began the dance of questions and answers.

"if you track the lines in the image in a state of tranquil contemplation,
the message within may begin to unfold."

—Blanche Merz

In Nazca, Peru, dancers danced lines into the desert,
for their desire to enter the earth and fecundate it.

To speak about a drawing displaces it,
undrawing it.

In displacement is discovery,
the beginning of transformation.

To "think" comes from *tong*, the common root of think, thank, feel,
pensar, agradecer, y sentir.

To think, *pensar*, in Romance languages is *pendere*, to weigh suspending a weight from a thread.

Her pendent thoughts asked, letting the pendulum guide her hand to transcribe the virtual plane,
the drawing landing on the page.

This is how she "saw" the invisible translating into line and color.

The "real" comes from *rei, riga* and line.

Geometry and alliance, something in us allies itself to the alignment.

"The arc of alliances with all its power"

—Violeta Parra

The sound of "thinking" is perhaps a shock, a transmission of the force of a message traveling through the sensory thread, dendrite and neuron.

Pentagrams of the infinite.

Pentagrams of relationships.

Musical scores.

"True music is musical thoughts"

—Hazrat Inayat Khan

I am listening to its fibers

a garden
of sounds

son (sound) (they are)

a singing
of strings
without strings

son (sound) (they are)

"Everything happens in accordance with a specific system of law"

—Emma Kunz

Dialogic works, her designs are both an answer and a question, an investigation of the "law."

"a law which I feel within me."

—Emma Kunz

Legere once meant to pick up.

The law is what is read, not in a text but in a life.

In the unchanging change.

Whichever word is read today is a con-densation, a moment in its transformation.

But how to read the law in a diagram and return it to act?

How to read feeling, not the drawing but its *enorgía*?

"There are no such things as miracles. It is the law.
It all depends whether we can work with it."

—Emma Kunz

Hilma af Klint speaks of co-laboring with the forces.

To work with, to become the companion of reflection, say the Guaraní.

Jechaka mba'ekuaá, the organ of sight, is the reflection of its wisdom, the birth of the sun and the creator's thought.

Theorem and theory of seeing, the reality of god is *theos*, a gaze.

"Diagram" is to cut and to separate scratches.

"Science" is to cut and "conscience" to unite and cut at the same time.

Two contradictory movements form a third.

Imagination's inception.

A drawing is but a trace of the imaginal.

A form is only a distant reflection of an initial shine.

Form is gleam, sparkle *reluciendo*.

To read the law is to ignite it with love,
like a lover who feeling loved returns love two-fold.

Violence and destruction are also repaid.
Every fiber of the weave dialogues and reverberates with others.

Harald Szeemann says:

"Her true task was to proclaim the possibilities of a life lived in the spirit."

A life lived!

"In the light," Emma Kunz is reported as saying, "there are billions of tiny dots. When these are caught against the light or discerned by a keen eye, they are multiplied—like a pregnancy."

"They also multiply of their own accord, so that there are immense numbers of good germs, seeds swarming in the air. Wherever these end up, is another body of light, important for the Earth and for the Universe."

Every cell, every form, emits light and is, like light, pregnant with itself.

NEW YORK, AUGUST 2001

Performance Notes

AUTHOR'S NOTE: Very late in the process of constructing *Spit Temple*, the book that Rosa Alcalá assembled, it occurred to me that she might want to see my "Performance Notes," handwritten drawings/scribblings/ texts that are the basis for my oral performances or "Quasars."

The notes explore or map the "field of composition" in which I find myself just before the performance. They often weave in the political or ecological disasters of the moment, the wars and violations of human rights haunting us. The Quasars and the performance notes represent a contemporary form of "hatun simi," the principal language of Quechua poetics based on the concept of "chantay simi": "to speak weaving," where I connect many languages and poetries to seed the transformation of the world.

Previously unpublished.

~ ~

NOTA DE LA AUTORA: Cuando el proceso de construcción de *Spit Temple,* el libro que armó Rosa Alcalá, estaba muy avanzado, pensé mostrarle mis "Performance Notes", una serie de apuntes/dibujos escritos a mano, que son la base de los performances orales, o quasares.

Las notas exploran o mapean el campo de composición en el que me encuentro antes del performance. A menudo tejen relatos de los desastres políticos y ecológicos, las guerras y violaciones de los derechos humanos que nos acosan. Los Quasares (o cuasares) y las notas de los performances representan una forma actual de "hatun simi" o lengua principal, un concepto quechua basado en la idea del "chantay simi": hablar tejiendo, aquí transformado en un canto multilingüe que conecta las lenguas y la poesía plantando una semilla para transformar el mundo.

I hereby ask permission
to enter into the light
of those sounds

the sounds of the ancients
I don't know how to pronounce
my not knowing the rudder
into their joy
my desire to join them
in the dance, the hunt
free dancing
with

el timón
il bel

soy
el fuego que
baila en las sombras

soy
soy   el fuego
en   sombra
          sombra
        la
soy

nacimiento del arco iris

había llegado el quiebre, (a la) caída, (el)serrucho de luz
al todo tragando oscuridad, una fuerza tan negra
y tirante, sediente y espesa, que todo chupaba
(a su)imán. y hoyo negro mental. centro del
cosmos, ahí, ibas a dar.   entonces, un quiebre

inhalado, un murmullo templado, se lió haciendo
luz, luz del sonido, dijo el algo, y le gustó. lo vio
dejó despedir su calor, su nota en sí menor
(su)nota en despliegue de amor dijo algo.
"amor"? nadie había oído el murmuro,
el remanente del rayo   "luz de amor", su
sonido tan pliegue   nadie lo oyó sonido
y el no oír, tembló, al mismo de luz
del rayo se oyó, un quiebre de luz
siguiendo el a rayo, el remedo del
rayo, en su variación. ¡ahí está
libro mío, dijo (el)algo, ¿compa-
rando su nacer, en ese instante
otro cedió su lugar, y el uno
borrarse otro nacía de su
quebrazón, ángulo vivo
serrucho hablador
el arco nació-
de un quiebre
de luz.

* un quejido
del pliegue

amigo del hoyo negro
temblor

su nota en sí,   armonía menor
del menor   del
armonía   medio
del tiempo
su nota
en despliegue
gusto y
más,
dijo
"esto
en amor"

el no oír
nació
de un
temblor

compañero
de mi
nacer

quiebre vivo
ángulo hablador

* en un dejo
de aplomo
un murmullo
de oro
un quiebre
templado,
se lió
haciendo
luz

nota
alterada
subiendo
el tono
libro mío-

* en ese instante
un quiebre

enter
necido
compañero
de mi
nacer-
y otro rayo
sin ruido
nació-
uno dejando
al otro ser
uno
se
otro

inventar
los rayos
de amor,
con pliegue
en los hoyos

CUNEIFORME EL UMBAL

cha ñun tj ku
linudo   tonudo

wallpa mawell
cuerpo una flecos torcidos (de)
nevados alzados

bordes de cuerpos

duwen mawell

cha ñun tj ku

flecos torcidos
en las mejillas
de la lluvia

mawun

lluvia de luna
el mawell

llueve tibio
llueve caliente
lloviendo fino

wallpa mawell chañuntuku

asoma sus dedos
negros
chiñai

---

düwen: lo tejido

en 3 reinos

el cuerpo   la casa   el cielo

ikülla   pontro   metra
iwutue   pichilama   kutama
makuñ   chañu
ñarüwe   chañuntuku
trarilonko
kepam
chiripa

wanglen kutama
alforja con estrellas

_____ es una metra *
(apero con sexo)
la asimetría es de
mujer
(usadas como chaspino)

sudadero se desteje del
pelero

Para montar el caballo
pillán
el que sube a los cielos
del rakiduam

por su wirin
sendero de estrellas
y truenos

---

la mía es trarikan lama
un textil erudito, ikat

es un tejido de uso universal
todos lo pueden tocar
ahí se "escriben"
se codifican los contenidos
que no deben ser olvidados.

se escriben en las estrellas

angel tetudo

* ángel de las escrituras
cuneiforme
"no muke"

umbra y umbral

palacio de sombras

escrit del ángel

lu pai!

bomb. | las tumbas

borrar el com.

nimrud

siqno
en la mano

ángel tetudo

cuneiforme
"no muke"

nimrud
escritura
cuneiforme
no muke

Pal e'nimrud

borrar el com
es se con
el final

sellar el final

em   p   ire

       is

    f   e   a   r

       is

    em   p   ire

    el   miedo

          es

    im   perio

imperio

    del

        miedo

    es

em   p   ire

       is

    f   e   a   r   of

i   m   p   e   r   i   o

          p

          e

          s

        el   m   iedo

em   p   i   re

       is

       of

    f   e   a   r

              of

arid   lacking moisture

L āridus   þarēre   ardere
           as   to burn
                     glow

OE   asœ   ash

L. ās-ī = āra
        altar

our dryness
our ash
our ora
    altar

arid
ash
altar

ardent ⎯⎯⎯⎯⎯⎯⎯

ardor ⎯⎯⎯⎯⎯⎯

en aras de la vida

arid
ardere
to burn
ash
altar

arid
ardent
ardor

en aras
de la v..

burn
ash

altar

Temu divericatum

Te mu co

apuas de temu

apuas de un árbol

que ora

y da vida

al que lava

sus ojos

en llas

a los

ojos

del

recién

nacido

desdoblamiento por corte

transformar / no representa

lu k v t v e l

pensamiento

acostado

figura de un

corte

por desdoblamiento

vertical.

ñi min

desmembran

deshacen

rompen

la imagen

para que nadie

la pueda

copiar

desolladas

dislocadas

des-articulan

lonko   cabeza

wi siwel cuerpo

piuke   corazón

ñi min es la carnicería

de la representación p.18

inner ecology

(Poetry is the mist

the bridge of sound

set the 2 laws of the forest

the "law of moderation" again in nature

"   "   "   inner mod = self vigilance

the life in the Forest

depended on   a metaphor
                               is the evidence
was supported by

        Poetry
        is the only   a living "
        proof of
        human   made alive   by
        ness
                         people's belief

The Forest is a collective Act
of self Knowledge
                         the chiripá
                              say

Endnotes

SABOR A MÍ/STUPID DIARY (1966–1971)

Misión/Research Project, written in April 1971, foretells the "Besatón por la educación," a collective kissing event performed by thousands of students to demand free education at the Plaza de Armas in Santiago, July 7, 2011. The poem was published for the first time in *El Zen Surado* by Cecilia Vicuña (Catalonia, 2013).

PALABRAR*mas* (1966–2015)

IN side the VISIBLE: M. Catherine de Zegher used this Palabrarmas for the title of her exhibition *Inside the Visible: An Elliptical Traverse of 20th Century Art in, of, and from the Feminine* (1996) at the ICA Boston: "an alternative reading of the traditional male-dominated view of 20th century art history" (Griselda Pollock), which presented previously "invisible" figures alongside established artists to create a re-theorized interpretation of the art of this century.

PRECARIO/PRECARIOUS (1966–2015)

Espiral y Mar/Spiral and Sea: The first spirals I created in Con cón can be seen in my film *Kon Kon* (www.konkon.cl).

Antivero: For my ongoing relationship to this mountain stream in the Colchagua region of Chile, see: https://vimeo.com/104533099.

Quipu Menstrual: The Pascua Lama mining project in Huasco, Atacama, has been temporarily stalled, but the struggle of the Diaguita people against the project continues. Despite the increasing desertification and drought in Chile, a new law that will authorize the destruction of the glaciers is currently under discussion in Congress. This follows the privatization of water and the disappearance of the water rights of the people.

Semiya: The Semiya project was re-created in Denmark, at the Kunsthal Aarhus (see #SEMIYA2015).

LA WIK'UÑA

Iridesce: The Greek word *iris,* from the Proto-Indo-European *wi-ri* means "to bend." It names the eye and the messenger. In the Andes, the iridescent hummingbird is the messenger of light, and reflections are prayers of light.

Guainambí Tominejo, The Last Hummingbird: The Andean hummingbird feeds on nectar (*nekrós,* "death" in Greek) and "dies" symbolically every night, going into torpor, so it plays a similar role to the Greek goddess Iris as a symbol for resurrection.

La sequencia del agua/The water sequence: In the Andes, water is the sacred thread of life from glacier to ocean and back.

Unuy Quita, "You, my lovely waters" (Quechua), echoes an Inka song constructed with lines of four syllables meant to act like water falling on rocks. From my perspective, "unuy" suggests the Spanish "una": one, stressing the unity of water, from sewage to watershed and back.

CLOUD-NET

Cloud-net was a traveling exhibition and a series of street performances dedicated to the Sixth Extinction caused by human activity and global warming. "Today, we face losing 30,000 species a year … the fastest mass extinction in Earth's 4.5-billion-year history. This time, however, it is mainly the result of human activity, not natural phenomena." (American Museum of Natural History.)

Er intertwines different translations of "The Fable of Er," an orphic myth in *The Iliad, The Odyssey,* and Plato's *The Republic.* A video of the three fates performance in *Er* is available at: vimeo.com/122567318.

Red Cabezal/Head Net sequence combines elements from the *Popol Vuh,* the Quiché Mayan book of creation translated by Dennis Tedlock, and *The Art of the Maya Scribe* by Michael D. Coe and Justin Kerr (1998). About the scribal god *paw ah tun,* Justin Kerr says: "In the *Cordamex* dictionary there is a gloss for *paw* as *talega de red,* and in fact, we often see the headdress being worn from the neck as a sack or bag." The *ah* personalizes the name in *ah tzib,* which changes the word from "to write" to that of "the writer or the artist." We see the "*ah*" in action in: *ah k'u hun,* scribe, *ts'ib,* writing and painting, *ah ts'ib,* he (she) of the writing and painting, *its'at,* artist. (Ibid.)

Illapantac, Illapa, one of the oldest deities in Andean myth, controls fluidity and rain. Its name condenses thunder, lightning, and thunderbolt. The supreme mediator of sound, it is also known as Pachacuti, "world reverser."

Dheu is the Proto-Indo-European root of the word "cloud." The poem refers to sweatshops and other textile factories in New York where immigrant workers are exploited.

EL TEMPLO/THE TEMPLE

K'ij means day in K'iche' Maya; *k'ijilabal,* to pray; and *k'ijiloxic,* to divine, or "be dayed." (Barbara Tedlock, *Time and the Highland Maya.*)

Tiempo/Time and temple share the common root *dai,* to divide: a space set apart for observation.

Nazca refers to a Nazca (100 B.C.–700 A.D.) ceramic, on which a woman represents herself tattooed with stars. Her body reminds me of the Nazca Lines and other star symbols tattooed on the earth along the southern coast of Peru and in northern Chile.

Muslo/Thigh: The Maya scribe appears to have a glyph on his/her thigh, perhaps from wiping the brush on it, incorporating the body into the work.

Adiano y Azúmbar/Ancient & Star Flowered: This poem combines the story of Huaca Purpur, a traveling dune that moves as a sign in the Viru desert valley of the north coast of Peru with the color purple (*púrpura* in Spanish) of the Manquehue mountain facing my bedroom in Santiago. Azúmbar is a plant whose fruit is shaped like a star. The movements of the dune, seen from space, sometimes take the shape of a star.

QUIPOem

Quipo, or quipu: knot in Quechua. A spatial system of annotation in knots and threads used for government statistics, poetic and musical (k)notation, and other recordkeeping in Inka and pre-Inka periods, going back 5,000 years.

Ceque (Quechua; also zeq'e) was a system of ritual pathways or sightlines radiating outward from Cuzco into the rest of the Inca Empire (15th century). Scholars are unclear as to its use or meaning. For me, the *ceque* is a virtual *quipu* connecting the body and the community to the cosmos and the sources of water in the mountains.

Allqa, the union of black and white, is a ritual Aymara concept used in weaving.

INSTAN

Alba saliva was written in a language between English and Spanish—not Spanglish, but what I call a *Cognado Potens*, a potential tongue emerging from the cognates these languages share. It represents a middle state of mind, equally readable or unreadable from both. While composing it, I could see the poem acted as a riddle, each word opening up to reveal ancient or future meanings. I realized *Instan* was *hatunsimi,* a Quechua concept meaning "a pregnant word that gives birth to many." (Diego González Holguín, *Vocabulario de la Lengua General de Todo el Peru, Llamada Lengua Quichua o del Inca*, Cuzco, 1608.) Another element of the composition is that the word "alba" (dawn) is a palindrome of "habla" (speech). For the Inka, generative words are often palindromes: *wiñay qallallallaq pacha*: the fertility of all generations. Alba/habla, the dawn of a new speech, is a movement in both directions.

SPIT TEMPLE

The Quasar: I began calling my performances "quasars" in the 1980s, since I see them as quasi-events. "In whatever direction we look into deep space … toward the observable horizon, we see only quasars—quasistellar objects—and the uniform glow of radio radiation from the big bang. Quasars, the most distant observable objects … the most curious and the most energetic." ("The Known Universe," *National Geographic Atlas of the World*, 1981.)

K'isa/alangó combines Aymara (k'isa) and Old Javanese (alangó) as parallel concepts of "beauty." K'isa is derived from Verónica Cereceda's 1987 essay, "Aproximaciones a una estética andina." "Alangó" is derived from the translation by P.J. Zoetmulder (1974) of ancient texts of the ninth-century A.D., quoted by Stephen Lansing. (Jerome Rothenberg and David Guss, eds., *The Book, Spiritual Instrument*, Granary Books, 1996.)

No Manifesto of The No Tribe*:* "Tribu No" was the name I gave to a group of friends, a gathering of poets and artists in Santiago in 1967. Together we conducted anonymous poetic actions in the city.

Woodland Pattern Book Center, Milwaukee, Wisconsin, September 29, 2001: For more on the death of Luis Gómez in New York City, July, 1998, see: http://www.nytimes.com/1998/07/12/nyregion/construction-worker-is-buried-alive-in-pit.html.

UNCOLLECTED POEMS

Libro Desierto/Desert Book refers to the Nazca Lines in the South Coast of Peru (100 B.C.–600 A.D.). The poem was inspired by Anthony Aveni and Helaine Silverman's narrative of the moment when Paul and Rose Kosok observed the lines on June 21, 1941.

Angel de las escrituras, cuneiforme el umbral/Angel of Writing, Cuneiform Threshold: On March 5, 2003, Ash Wednesday, artists gathered in the Metropolitan Museum in New York to protest the Iraq war by sketching works of ancient Mesopotamia. When I arrived the room was filled with people sitting on the floor, quietly drawing fragments of scripts found on reliefs from the palace of ancient Nimrud. Meanwhile, scholars from all over the world were entreating the Pentagon to protect Iraq's ruins and museums, which held humanity's patrimony: the dawn of writing and civilization. None of these gestures, however, prevented the barbaric assault unleashed by the invasion, the looting of museums, and the burning of Baghdad's national library and archive. The poem refers to Angel #11, from the threshold of the Assyrian palace of Ashurnasirpal II at Nimrud in northern Mesopotamia, ninth-century C.E., at the Metropolitan Museum.

Des pedida/Leave Taking transcribes words spoken by Gerónima Sequeida, the great singer of *bagualas* of Amaicha del Valle in Tucumán, Argentina. They were compiled by Leda Valladares and Leopoldo

Brizuela. The "baile de empellejados" is a ritual dance also practiced across the Andes, in Chile. See: http://www.contenidoslocales.cl/content/30203/baile-de-los-empellejados-de-lora-parte-1.

Oir es el oro/To Hear Is to Strike Gold is my response to the Pascua Lama mining project in Atacama, Chile, currently destroying the glaciers that feed the Valle del Huasco. See: http://www.quipumenstrual.cl.

Quen-to Shipibo is based on the aesthetic concepts of the *kikin ainbo*, or cultivated women, of the Shipibo-Conibo of the Upper Amazon, whose art reveals *shina*, depth of imagination and thought. These artists name their expressions *quen-* which means to love, to desire. Their art is focused on *kikin*, the efficacy and beauty of the visible and invisible designs that sustain the world. (Angelika Gebhart-Sayer, *The Cosmos Encoiled: Indian Art of the Peruvian Amazon*, Americas Society, 1984.)

Mete o rito: Agustina Quinchamal (1875?–1950?), a Tehuelche artist and "interpreter" (*lenguaraza*) from Argentina, spoke seven languages, painted abstract designs on guanaco hides, and sang. One of the songs she sang, having lost her four children, was a Kani myth of the mother turned meteorite:

"Ahora qué hago?	(Now what do I do?)
Mi hijo se empantanó.	(My son has drowned in the marsh.)
O me vuelvo monte	(Either I become a mountain)
O me vuelvo piedra."	(Or I turn to stone.)

In 1896 Francisco P. Moreno "discovered" the actual meteorite, considered sacred by the Tehuelche, which was moved later to the Museo de La Plata in Argentina.

When she visited El Museo de la Plata in 1949, at the request of her friend the ethnographer Federico Escalada, to "identify" or check out the names and categories of the Tehuelche "objects" in their collection, they decided to photograph her braids, turning her into another object.

Disprosodias alters the words written by Xul Solar in the 1920s. It was commissioned by Lila Zemborain for the exhibition and book catalog of the exhibition *Xul Solar and Jorge Luis Borges: The Art of Friendship* at the Americas Society, New York, 2013. For more on Xul Solar, see: http://www.wordswithoutborders.org/article/co-ecos-astri-xul-solar-of-buenos-aires.

The Melody of Structures was revised from Rosa Alcalá's translation of my poem-essay commissioned by M. Catherine de Zegher for 3× *Abstraction: New Methods of Drawing by Hilma Af Klint, Emma Kunz, and Agnes Martin*, Yale University Press (New Haven, 2005). Quotes are drawn from: *Emma Kunz: Artist, Researcher, Natural Healer* (Emma Kunz Zentrum, Würenlos, 1998).

Photo Credits

GESTURES

1. *The Glove*, Chile 1966–New York, 2011. Performance by Cecilia Vicuña. Photo by Robert Kolodny.

2. *Con Con*, Chile, 2006. Site-specific performance installation by Cecilia Vicuña. Photo by James O'Hern.

3. *Palabrarma*, London, 1974. Ink drawing by Cecilia Vicuña.

4. *Brooklyn Waterfall*, New York, 1994. Site-specific performance installation by Cecilia Vicuña. Photo by César Paternosto.

5. *Bogotá Poncho, (Sendero Chibcha)*, Bogotá, 1981. Site-specific performance installation by Cecilia Vicuña. Photo by Oscar Monsalve.

6. *Violeta Parra*, Bogotá, 1976. Ink drawing by Cecilia Vicuña.

7. *Cloud-net*, DiverseWorks, Houston, Texas, 1999. Site-specific performance installation by Cecilia Vicuña. Photo by Kim Thompson.

8. *Hands holding people*, Bogotá, 1976. Ink drawing by Cecilia Vicuña.

9. *Tunquén*, 1981. Site-specific performance installation by Cecilia Vicuña. Photo by Ricardo Vicuña.

10. *Self Portrait As Maya Scribe*, Bogotá, 1976. Ink drawing by Cecilia Vicuña.

11. *Writing/Drawing on Sand*, Con Con, Chile, 1966. Site-specific performance installation by Cecilia Vicuña.

12. *Bogotá typewriter*, 1976. Site-specific performance installation by Cecilia Vicuña. Photographer unknown.

13. *Cloud Baby*, DiverseWorks, Houston, Texas, 1999. Site-specific performance installation by Cecilia Vicuña. Photo by Kim Thompson.

14. *Sol de Rari*, New York, 2013. Site-specific performance installation by Cecilia Vicuña. Photo by Maricruz Alarcón.

10 METAPHORS IN SPACE

1. *Espiral y mar*, Con Con, Chile, 2016. Site-specific performance installation by Cecilia Vicuña. Photo by James O'Hern.

2. *Otoño*, Santiago, Chile, 1971–1978. Site-specific performance installation by Cecilia Vicuña. Photo by Carlos Baeza.

3. *Antivero*, Colchagua, Chile, 1981. Site-specific performance installation by Cecilia Vicuña. Photo by César Paternosto.

4. *Guante*, Santiago, Chile, 1966–1994. Site-specific performance installation by Cecilia Vicuña. Photo by Catherine de Zegher.

5. *Vaso de Leche*, Bogotá, 1979. Site-specific performance installation by Cecilia Vicuña. Photo by Oscar Monsalve.

6. *Galaxia de Basura*, New York, 1989. Site-specific performance installation by Cecilia Vicuña. Photo by César Paternosto.

7. *Shadow of a Loom*, New York, 1993. Site-specific performance installation by Cecilia Vicuña. Photo by César Paternosto.

8. *Quipu Menstrual*, Nevado del Plomo, Chile, 2006. Site-specific performance installation by Cecilia Vicuña. Photo by James O'Hern.

9. *Río Mapocho*, Santiago, 2012, Chile. Site-specific performance installation by Cecilia Vicuña. Photo by Matías Cardone.

10. *Semiya*, Chile 2000–Aarhus, 2015. Site-specific performance installation by Cecilia Vicuña. Photo by the artist.

DRAWINGS BY CECILIA VICUÑA

1. *Palabrarmas*, London, 1974. Ink on paper, p. 66–67

2. *Palabrarmas*, London, 1974. Ink and pencil on paper, p. 78–79

3. *Guitarra de boca, Violeta Parra*, Bogotá, 1977. Pencil on paper, p. 144–145

4. *El torturador*, Bogotá, 1977. Pencil on paper, p. 190–191

5. *Autoretrato como escriba maya*, Bogotá, 1976, p. 225

6. *Com, compassion compass*, New York, 2000, p. 228

7. *Com panion com miserate*, New York, 2000, p. 229

8. *Am ma*, New York, 2000, p. 250

9. *Wobbly drawing, Shipibo Conibo bordado translation*, New York, 2018. Pencil on paper, p. 309

10. *Performance notes*, New York, 1990's–2006, p. 343–351

Biographical Notes

CECILIA VICUÑA is a poet, artist, filmmaker and activist. Her work addresses pressing concerns of the modern world, including ecological destruction, human rights, and cultural homogenization. Born and raised in Santiago de Chile, she has been in exile since the early 1970s, after the military coup against elected president Salvador Allende. Vicuña began creating "precarious works" in the mid 1960s in Chile as a way of "hearing an ancient silence waiting to be heard." Her multi-dimensional works begin as a poem, an image that morphs into a film, a song, a sculpture, or a collective performance. These ephemeral, site-specific installations in nature, streets, and museums combine ritual and assemblage. She calls these impermanent, participatory acts "lo precario" (the precarious). A partial list of museums that have exhibited her work includes: The National Museum of Contemporary Art (EMST), Athens, Greece; documenta-Halle, Kassel, Germany; The Museu de Arte Moderna do Rio de Janeiro, Brazil; The Museo Nacional de Bellas Artes de Santiago; The Institute of Contemporary Arts (ICA), London; The Contemporary Arts Center (CAC), New Orleans; The Whitechapel Art Gallery in London; The Berkeley Art Museum; The Whitney Museum of American Art; and MoMA, The Museum of Modern Art in New York.

Vicuña has published twenty-two art and poetry books, including *Read Thread, The Story of the Red Thread* (Sternberg Press, 2017), *About to Happen* (Siglio, 2017), *Kuntur Ko* (Tornsound, 2015), *Spit Temple: The Selected Performances of Cecilia Vicuña* (Ugly Duckling Presse, 2012), *Instan* (Kelsey Street Press, 2001) and *Cloud Net* (Art in General, 2000). In 2009, she co-edited *The Oxford Book of Latin American Poetry: 500 years of Latin American Poetry*. She edited *ÜL: Four Mapuche Poets* in 1997. She was appointed Messenger Lecturer 2015 at Cornell University, and participated in documenta 14, in Athens and Kassel in 2017. She divides her time between Chile and New York.

www.ceciliavicuna.com   www.konkon.cl   www.oysi.com

ROSA ALCALÁ is a recipient of an NEA Literary Translation Fellowship, and has published translations of poetry by Cecilia Vicuña, Lila Zemborain, Lourdes Vázquez, and others. Her translations also appear in the anthologies *The Oxford Book of Latin American Poetry* and *Angels of the Americlypse: An Anthology of New Latin@ Writing*. *Spit Temple: The Selected Performances of Cecilia Vicuña*, edited and translated by Alcalá, was runner-up for a PEN Award for Poetry in Translation. Her third book of poetry, *MyOTHER TONGUE*, was published in 2017. She lives in El Paso, TX, where she teaches in the Department of Creative Writing/Bilingual MFA Program at the University of Texas-El Paso.

ESTHER ALLEN teaches at the Graduate Center and Baruch College, City University of New York. Her most recent translation is *Zama*, by Antonio Di Benedetto (New York Review Books Classics). She is currently at work on a biography of José Martí.

SUZANNE JILL LEVINE, professor of Latin American and Comparative Literature and director of Translation Studies at the University of California in Santa Barbara, is currently translating Eduardo Lalo's *La inutilidad* for University of Chicago Press. Noted translator, and author of the literary biography *Manuel Puig and the Spider Woman: His Life and Fictions* and *The Subversive Scribe: Translating Latin American Fiction*, her most recent honor is a PEN award in 2012 for her translation of José Donoso's *The Lizard's Tale*.

EDWIN MORGAN (1920–2010) was born and educated in Glasgow, where he returned to lecture in English Literature at Glasgow University after a period in the army. He was the author of many books, including poetry, criticism, essays, translations, plays, and works of concrete poetry, for which he received awards including the Queen's Gold Medal for Poetry and the Weidenfeld Prize for Translation. He was the first Glasgow Poet Laureate and the first Scottish national poet: The Scots Makar.

URAYOÁN NOEL is the author of six books of poetry, most recently *Buzzing Hemisphere/Rumor Hemisférico* (Arizona), a *Library Journal* Top Fall Indie Poetry selection. His other books include the critical study *In Visible Movement: Nuyorican Poetry from the Sixties to Slam* (Iowa), winner of the LASA Latino Studies Book Prize, and the bilingual edition *Architecture of Dispersed Life: Selected Poems by Pablo de Rokha*, forthcoming from Shearsman. Noel has received fellowships from the Ford Foundation, the Howard Foundation, and CantoMundo. Originally from Puerto Rico and based in the Bronx, he teaches at NYU and at the low-residency MFA of the Americas at Stetson University.

JAMES O'HERN was born in Laredo, Texas, on April 17, 1933. He studied at Southern Methodist University, the University of California at Los Angeles, and New York University Graduate School of Business. O'Hern is the author of *Honoring the Stones* (Curbstone Press, 2004). He is also a filmmaker and has collaborated with the performance artist and poet Cecilia Vicuña on multiple projects. With Vicuña, he is the president and cofounder of Oysi, Inc., a nonprofit organization helping indigenous cultures preserve their poetic traditions. He lives in New York City.

ANNE TWITTY has dedicated herself to the study and diffusion of spiritual traditions in many forms, including poetry. Her collaboration with Iraj Anvar, *Say Nothing: Poems of Jalal al-Din Rumi in Persian and English*, appeared in 2008. Previously, she had received the PEN Prize for Poetry in Translation in 2002 and an NEA translation grant in 2006. For some years she was Epicycle Editor of *Parabola Magazine*, which published her retellings of traditional stories and her original writings.

ELIOT WEINBERGER's books of literary essays include *Karmic Traces, An Elemental Thing*, and *The Ghosts of Birds*. His political articles are collected in *What I Heard About Iraq* and *What Happened Here: Bush Chronicles*. The author of *19 Ways of Looking at Wang Wei*, he is a translator of the poetry of Bei Dao, the editor of *The New Directions Anthology of Classical Chinese Poetry*, and the general editor of the series *Calligrams: Writings from and on China*. He is also the literary editor of the Murty Classical Library of India. Among his many translations of Latin American literature are *The Poems of Octavio Paz*, Jorge Luis Borges' *Selected Non-Fictions*, and Vicente Huidobro's *Altazor*.

CHRISTOPHER WINKS is Associate Professor of Comparative Literature at Queens College/CUNY. He is the author of *Symbolic Cities in Caribbean Literature* (Palgrave-Macmillan, 2009), and his essays, reviews, and translations from French and Spanish have appeared in numerous journals and edited collections. Recent translations include Juan Bosch's *Social Composition of the Dominican Republic* (Routledge), *Labyrinth*, a selection from the writings of Cuban poet Lorenzo García Vega (Junction Press), and *Soft Matter*, a serial poem by Lila Zemborain.